ROUGH GUIDES

T0082470

POCKET **ROUGH GUIDE**
SEVILLE

written and researched by
MEGAN LLOYD & JOANNA REEVES

CONTENTS

SEVILLE

"Seville has a special colour," goes the popular song by Los del Río. And who, after laying eyes on the pastel facades, rainbow of tiles and thousands of orange trees lining the cobblestone streets, would ever disagree? Seville has many important monuments and an illustrious history, but what it's essentially famous for is its own living self – the greatest city of the Spanish south, of Carmen, Don Juan and Figaro, and the archetype of Andalusian promise. This reputation for gaiety and brilliance, for theatricality and intensity of life is well deserved. It's expressed on a phenomenally grand scale at the city's two great festivals – Semana Santa (Holy Week at Easter) and the Feria de Abril (which starts two weeks after Easter Sunday and lasts a week) – and in the delicious minutiae of daily life, which is slow, celebratory and centred on food, drink and soaking up the sun.

Magnificent gardens of the Alcázar

With an economy powered by the likes of food and tobacco processing, chemical manufacturing and aircraft construction, Seville lies at the centre of a humble agricultural region surrounded by an endless sea of olive groves and citrus orchards. The total refurbishment of the infrastructure boosted by the '92 World Expo – including impressive new roads, seven bridges, a high-speed rail link and a revamped airport – helped regenerate the city's (and the region's) fortunes, and built the foundation for a robust tourism sector. There is still much work to be done in terms of modern economic growth, but fortunately for travellers, Seville's traditional way of living and connection to both the culture and land is part of the city's charm.

Seville's shopping artery, Calle Sierpes

Convent cookies

Roaming the city in the early hours and suddenly overcome with an intense craving for cookies? That could be down to the sweet scent of sugar and spice wafting from Seville's convents. Baking has long been a tradition of Spanish nuns since the fifteenth century, especially for those who were cloistered and unable to leave the grounds. What makes Spain's holy sweets especially interesting is the addition of honey, almonds and warm spices like ginger, cloves and anis – a nod to the culinary influence of both Jewish and Moorish communities. Many convents still retain the traditional turntable point of sale designed to keep the sisters out of public view: you place your cash and order in a revolving counter called a *torno*, which then rotates to reveal your chosen bag of goodies on the other side. It can be challenging to figure out which churches sell baked goods and what to try. The following are a good place to start – just show up early so you don't miss the treats:

Convento de Madre de Dios, C/San José 4. Try: marzipan *naranjitos* (nutty marzipan balls) and *bocaditos árabes* (cinnamon-spiked biscuits).

Monasterio de Santa Paula, C/Santa Paula 11. Try: *alfajores mozárabes* (almond cookies).

Convento de Santa Inés, C/Doña María Coronel 5. Try: sesame *bollitos* (buns) and *tortas de aceite* (anise biscuits).

Convento de San Leandro, Pza. San Ildefonso 1. Try: *yemas* ("egg yolks", a rich sugar-dusted pastry).

The colourful facades of Triana

Seville has long inspired creativity, with a rich heritage spanning traditional ceramics, music and flamenco through to contemporary art and design. The city has hosted some of the world's finest operas, including *The Marriage of Figaro*, *Carmen*, *The Barber of Seville* and *Don Giovanni*, and these spine-tingling masterpieces can be seen at the Teatro de la Maestranza. The world-class Museo de Bellas Artes de Sevilla shelters the works of Baroque masters and Renaissance painters, while ahead-of-the-curve galleries like Centro Andaluz de Arte Contemporáneo provide a platform for emerging talent. Seville has a thriving food scene, though it's less about collecting Michelin stars than embracing a culinary tradition that's withstood the test of time. The streets are littered with over three thousand tapas bars where locals jostle for space at time-worn counters, picking at plates of *pescaítos fritos* (fried fish), *espinacas con garbanzos* (spinach and chickpeas) and wafer-thin *jamón ibericó bellota*.

Seville's layered history is etched into the ancient stones of its old city: a jigsaw of Moorish, Christian and Islamic architecture the legacy of different rulers over the years. At the heart of the Centro Histórico stand three great monuments side by side: La Giralda, a minaret turned tower with fine views from its crown; the Catedral, the world's largest Gothic church and home to a staggering altarpiece; and the Alcázar, a magnificent royal palace where Moorish, Gothic, Mudéjar and Renaissance styles collide to glorious effect.

To the east unfurls Santa Cruz, the medieval Jewish quarter. Here, a tangle of narrow alleyways is

What's new

The Reales Atarazanas in the Arenal neighbourhood is set to open in 2024 as the city's largest collection of contemporary art, replacing the current Centro Andaluz de Arte Contemporáneo (CAAC) over in La Cartuja across the river. The new cultural centre, whose original structure served as the city's shipyard back in 1254 and, later, as an artillery factory, is looking to compete with the modern art offerings of the likes of Madrid. Additionally, the city has been slowly cleaning up each of the four facades of the emblematic Giralda tower since 2017. Each side takes about a full year to restore (there was a pause during the pandemic), and it's looking like the entire project will be completed by 2024.

lined by whitewashed houses hidden behind clouds of flowering plants. The beauty of the district has stirred the imagination of many an artist, most famously *barrio* resident Murillo and Valdés Leal, who painted the Baroque frescoes adorning the Hospital de los Venerables.

North of here is the main shopping and commercial district, its most obvious landmarks Plaza Nueva, Plaza del Duque de la Victoria and the smart, pedestrianized Calle Sierpes, which runs roughly between them. From La Campana, the small square at the northern end of Calle Sierpes, Calle Trajano takes you to the sprawling Alameda, a previously rundown area now known as one the city's hippest neighbourhoods, peppered with vintage shops, cool restaurants and a lively nightlife attracting a young crowd. West of here, the San Lorenzo *barrio* squats in the shadow of a revered church, its web of lanes untangling onto grand thoroughfares.

Also from La Campana, Calle Alfonso XII runs down towards the river by way of the Museo de Bellas Artes, second in cultural importance in Spain only to the Prado in Madrid. Across the Río Guadalquivir is the charismatic Triana *barrio*, the historic home of artisans, bullfighters and flamenco dancers, flanked to the south by Los Remedios, the city's wealthier neighbourhood where Seville's biggest street party – the riotous Feria de Abril – takes place every year in April.

The streets of Los Remedios come to life during Feria de Abril

Seville is home to 3000-plus tapas bars

While Seville is the fourth-largest city in Spain, its labyrinth-like streets can – and should – be explored on foot. Locals spill out onto the cobblestones from the sea of bars at all hours of the day, with an icy cold beer in one hand and a tapa in the other. In the orange tree-shaded plazas, kids kick around footballs after school, buskers perform soul-wrenching flamenco, and gaggles of *abuelas* sit waving off the afternoon sun with decorated fans.

If you'd rather explore on two wheels, the city is crisscrossed with over 180km of cycle lanes – part of Seville's push for a more sustainable approach to travel as the 2023 European Capital of Smart Tourism. Hire a bike and peddle through Parque de María Luisa, weaving around bubbling fountains and pretty gazebos, or venture to Alamillo Park on the Isla de la Cartuja.

Whether on foot or by bike, part of the joy of discovering Seville is to simply abandon your map and lose yourself in the tangle of pastel-washed alleyways, stumbling across handsome mansions, picturesque patios, dinky tapas bars and traditional shops where artisans still tinker away as they have done for years.

When to go

To avoid the sweltering summer months where locals shutter shops, head to the beach and practically abandon the city, stay out of Seville during June, July and August. If you are in town, make sure to find an indoor activity between the hours of 2pm and 8pm. Otherwise, Seville's temperate weather is precisely what lures tapas-goers and travellers to its festive streets throughout the year. Spring is surely the best time to visit the city, especially if you can catch the orange flowers in bloom, which fill the air with an intoxicating perfume signaling the beginning of the season. The autumn months are just as mild and lovely, and even winter is a delightful travel escape for folks living in frigid temperatures.

Where to...

Shop

Calle Sierpes and Calle Tetuán, two parallel pedestrianized streets in the centre, are the city's main shopping arteries, flanked by high-street brands and big-name boutiques. Be sure to duck down the sidestreets shooting off these bustling thoroughfares to browse smaller independent stores and gawk at elaborate flamenco dress shops. At Plaza del Duque de la Victoria, you will also find Spain's most-beloved department store, El Corte Inglés, crammed with both high-end designers and wallet-friendly brands. For more locally owned shops, check out the Alfalfa neighbourhood where you can buy handmade jewellery, clothing, art and crafts.
OUR FAVOURITES: La Importadora, see page 37; Tenderete, see page 37; Toni Pons, see page 38.

Eat

Seville seems to have more restaurants than people – locals practically live in the streets, eating and drinking from morning to night. But much like most cities in Spain, the main drag is the last place you want to sit down for a meal. Instead, venture off the touristed thoroughfares to stumble across small tapas bars packed with *sevillanos*. There are loads of traditional haunts scattered throughout the Arenal district, and a wider choice of cuisines as you move north towards Alameda. But the reality is, there's always a delicious bite waiting to be devoured in every corner of the city.
OUR FAVOURITES: El Bodeguita de Romero, see page 38; Eslava, see page 70; Señor Cangrejo, see page 40.

Drink

Like restaurants, there's no shortage of bars in Seville, from funky wine shops to fun rooftop spots with coveted views of La Giralda. Alameda has a high concentration of casual bars where you'll find young folks sipping beers or affordable gin and tonics late into the night. But don't miss the rooftop hotel bars in the old town, or the lively watering holes that line the Río Guadalquivir.
OUR FAVOURITES: Lama La Uva, see page 40; Muelle New York, see page 55; Pura Vida Terraza, see page 40.

Go out

Whether you're after live music, a soul-stirring flamenco performance or a rowdy night on the town, Seville is a fantastic place to go out. Alameda has a great spread of bars with live bands and DJs, many of which are LGBTQ+ friendly – here, you can dance into the wee hours of the morning. Paseo de Cristóbal Colón, a block off the river near the Triana Bridge, is another hotspot peppered with outdoor terraces and lively clubs. Just keep in mind that the latter rarely sees a crowd until well past midnight.
OUR FAVOURITES: La Carbonería, see page 49; Fun Club, see page 71; Maruja Melón, see page 62.

Seville at a glance

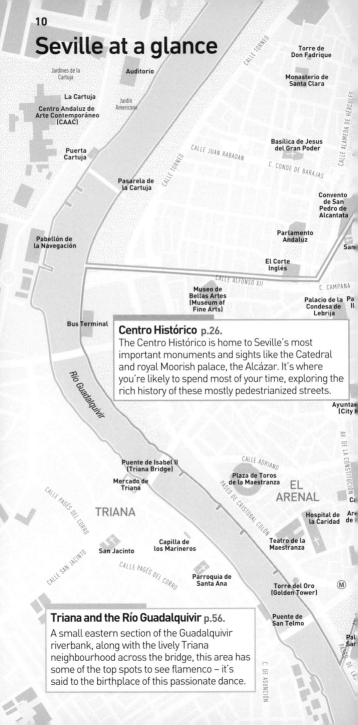

Jardines de la Cartuja

Auditorio

CALLE TORNEO

Torre de Don Fadrique

Monasterio de Santa Clara

La Cartuja

Jardín Americano

CALLE ALAMEDA DE HÉRCULES

Centro Andaluz de Arte Contemporáneo (CAAC)

Puerta Cartuja

CALLE JUAN RABADAN

Basílica de Jesus del Gran Poder

C. CONDE DE BARAJAS

Pasarela de la Cartuja

CALLE TORNEO

Convento de San Pedro de Alcantata

Parlamento Andaluz

San

Pabellón de la Navegación

El Corte Inglés

CALLE ALFONSO XII

C. CAMPANA

Museo de Bellas Artes (Museum of Fine Arts)

Bus Terminal

Palacio de la Condesa de Lebrija

Pa ll

Centro Histórico p.26.

The Centro Histórico is home to Seville's most important monuments and sights like the Catedral and royal Moorish palace, the Alcázar. It's where you're likely to spend most of your time, exploring the rich history of these mostly pedestrianized streets.

Río Guadalquivir

Ayunta (City

AV. DE LA CONSTITUCIÓN

Puente de Isabel II (Triana Bridge)

CALLE ADRIANO

Mercado de Triana

Plaza de Toros de la Maestranza

PASEO DE CRISTOBAL COLÓN

EL ARENAL

CALLE PAGÉS DEL CORRO

TRIANA

Ca

Hospital de la Caridad

Are de

CALLE SAN JACINTO

Capilla de los Marineros

San Jacinto

Teatro de la Maestranza

CALLE PAGÉS DEL CORRO

Parroquia de Santa Ana

Torre del Oro (Golden Tower)

Ⓜ

Triana and the Río Guadalquivir p.56.

A small eastern section of the Guadalquivir riverbank, along with the lively Triana neighbourhood across the bridge, this area has some of the top spots to see flamenco – it's said to the birthplace of this passionate dance.

Puente de San Telmo

Pal Sar

PASEO DE LA

C. DE ASUNCIÓN

Parroquia de San Gil

Convento de los Capuchinos

CALLE DE SAN LUIS

Murallas

lo de a

Palacio de los Marqueses de la Algaba

esia Omnium Sanctorum

Iglesia de San Luis de los Franceses

CALLE DE SAN LUIS

Convento de Santa Isabel

Alameda, San Lorenzo and Macarena p.64.

You'll find some of the most creative restaurants, bustling bars and spirited clubs in this district, along with off-the-beaten-path discoveries like venerated Catholic symbols and an aristocratic mansion.

Convento de Santa Paula

Escuelas Salesianas

CALLE DE CASTELLAR

an Juan la Palma

San Marcos

CALLE MARÍA AUXILIADORA

FONTANAL

n

Palacio de las Dueñas

CALLE BUSTOS TAVERA

CENTRO

Santa Catalina

CALLE ESCUELAS PIAS

CALLE RECAREDO

Las Setas (Metropol Parasol) San Pedro

unciación

Convento San Leandro

Casa de Pilatos

Colegial del o Salvador

San Ildefonso

C. AGUILAS

San Esteban

C. SAN ESTEBAN

CALLE RECAREDO

Museo del Baile Flamenco (Flamenco Dance Museum)

Santa Cruz p.42.

The picturesque Jewish quarter along the Alcázar is by far the most beautiful neighbourhood in Seville, with its web of cobblestoned paths, pastel-hued facades, hidden plazas and clouds of colourful flora.

SANTA CRUZ

Iglesia de Santa María la Blanca

acio ispal

Santa Cruz

C. STA. MARÍA LA BLANCA

Hospital de los Venerables

Museo Casa Murillo

CALLE DEMETRIO DE LOS RÍOS

Alcázar

Monumento a Colón

Jardines de Murillo (Murillo Gardens)

Sur p.50.

The South, with its wider boulevards, offers expansive spaces for open-air sights like the Plaza de España and the city's biggest natural hideaway, the Parque de María Luisa.

AN FERNANDO

Bus Terminal

Universidad de Sevilla

Antigua Fábrica de Tabacos

M

ro Lope de Vega

Jardines del Prado de San Sebastián

AVENIDA DE CARLOS V

Estación de San Bernardo

M

15

Things not to miss

While you can't see it all in just one visit, prioritizing these spots will give you a thorough insight into the best of Seville's history, art and culture.

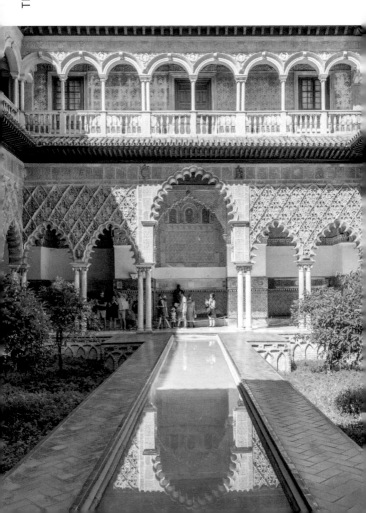

> **The Catedral**
See page 26
Built upon the base of a mosque, Seville's Catedral is the largest Gothic church in the world.

< **The Alcázar**
See page 32
This pristinely conserved Mudéjar palace, with its intricate carvings and vibrant gardens, nods to the long Moorish reign in the city.

∨ **La Giralda**
See page 27
Attached to the cathedral, this high-reaching former minaret is a towering emblem of the city.

< Córdoba
See page 86

Visit this charming Andalusian town, tucked into a crook in the Guadalquivir and home to the grandest mosque ever built by the Moors in Spain.

∨ Santa Cruz
See page 42

Seville's ancient Jewish quarter, with picturesque cobblestone streets winding beneath whitewashed houses punctuated by flower-adorned balconies.

< **Plaza de España**
See page 51
An impressive display of traditional *sevillano* architecture and design, with a romantic canal running from one end to the other.

∨ **Torre del Oro**
See page 57
Looming proudly over the Río Guadalquivir, this golden-hued tower houses a maritime museum plus views worthy of a riverside sentinel.

∧ Las Setas
See page 33
A modern mushroom-shaped structure boasts some of the best views of the city.

‹ Plaza de Toros
See page 36
Seville's famous bullring, complete with museum dedicated to the spectacle, is still active today.

∧ Antigua Fábrica de Tabacos
See page 50
With a fortress-like structure, this 1750s-built former tobacco factory contributed to Seville's wealth from a monopoly on trade with America. The inspiration for Bizet's famous *Carmen*, it's now home to the University of Seville.

∨ Museo de Bellas Artes
See page 35
One of the country's most impressive collections of art is housed in a beautiful former convent and showcases Baroque masterpieces, plus paintings from the Middle Ages, Renaissance and nineteenth century.

∧ Triana Bridge
See page 57
Officially named the Puente de Isabel II, this nineteenth-century bridge is the gateway to the vibrant Triana *barrio* and offers sublime views.

< Iglesia Colegial del Divino Salvador
See page 36
The second-largest church in Seville after the Catedral and one of the city's most elaborate displays of Baroque architecture.

< Archivo de Indias
See page 30
Browse some of the original documents connected to Spain's colonization of the Americas, stored in a sixteenth-century UNESCO-listed building.

∨ Casa de Pilatos
See page 43
One of the finest remaining aristocratic mansions in the city, with dazzling *azulejos*, a spectacular sixteenth-century stairway and an elegant patio.

THINGS NOT TO MISS

Day one in Seville

Alcázar. See page 32. Set aside a full morning to wander through the royal halls and magnificent gardens of Seville's grand Alcázar – a thirteenth-century Christian palace built over an Islamic castle. Gothic, Romanesque and Renaissance styles sit among Islamic ornamentation in this Mudéjar masterpiece.

Lunch. See page 48. With cured *jamón* curtaining the bar, *Casa Román* is a much-welcomed traditional tapas bar in a sea of tourist-leaning restaurants.

Santa Cruz. See page 42. Meander through the tangle of cobblestone streets, whitewashed houses and orange tree-shaded squares of the Jewish quarter.

Antigua Fábrica de Tabacos. See page 50. Head through the Jardínes de Murillo to explore the historic tobacco factory responsible for much of Seville's phenomenal wealth, and inspiration for iconic opera *Carmen*.

Plaza de España. See page 51. It took local architect Aníbal González a whopping fifteen years to complete this ambitious commission, built for the '29 Expo. Look out for the series of bold hand-painted tiles adorning the walls of this magnificent marvel, which tells the story of significant events in Seville's history.

Parque de María Luisa. See page 51. Escape the searing sun with a visit to this ficus-shaded park, wandering along leafy paths past perfectly manicured gardens and tranquil duck ponds.

Dinner. See page 55. Reserve a table at *Sobretablas*, where chef Camila Ferraro reimagines traditional Andalusian cuisine.

The Alcázar: a Mudéjar masterpiece

Plaza de España

Sobretablas

Day two in Seville

Las Setas. See page 33. Rub shoulders with locals at the city's favourite food market, Mercado de Encarnación, before hopping on the elevator to the top of "The Mushroom" for excellent views over the city.

The Catedral. See page 26. The largest Gothic church in the world is the final resting place of Christopher Columbus – or, at least, a part of him.

La Giralda. See page 27. Scale the magnificent bell tower, whose minaret nods to the church's original role as a mosque.

Mercado de Encarnación at Las Setas

Lunch. See page 38. Order a bunch of classic tapas to share at *El Bodeguita de Romero*, an unassuming neighbourhood haunt with a loyal following.

Museo de Bellas Artes. See page 35. Golden Age masterpieces by revered Spanish artists like Murillo, El Greco and Velásquez steal the show at Seville's excellent Museum of Fine Arts.

Triana Bridge. See page 57. Trace the curve of the Río Guadalquivir and head over the Puente de Isabel II into Triana, a dynamic enclave known for its rich heritage of flamenco and traditional craftmanship of ceramics.

CasaLa Teatro. See page 63. There's no better spot to catch a soul-stirring flamenco performance than this intimate *tablao* tucked away in the bustling Triana Market.

La Giralda

Dinner. See page 62. Fight your way to the bar counter at *Las Golondrinas* and shout out your order to the hurried servers; the salt-flecked pork tenderloin and the aioli-filled mushrooms are an absolute must.

Triana Bridge

Foodie Seville

Loosen your belt a couple of notches and follow your nose to Seville's most tantalizing cafés, speciality shops and fine-dining restaurants.

El Comercio. See page 38. Kick off the day with the city's finest churros dunked in a mug of hot chocolate; order to go if you're in a rush. If you have time to spare, join the queue for a table and try locals' favourite: toast with olive oil, tomato and cured ham.

Corta y Cata. See page 33. If you want to recreate the venerated breakfast toast (see above), this *jamón ibérico* shop in the Mercado de Encarnación sells excellent cured ham from nearby farms.

Convent cookies. See page 5. Convents around town are fronted by discrete stores where you can indulge in the nuns' famed sweet treats. The anise-flecked cookies are a must-try.

Freiduría Puerta de la Carne. See page 48. Seville's most famous fry shop may look unassuming from the outside, but its fried fish is legendary in these parts; the sunny patio is a perfect lunch spot.

Lama La Uva. See page 40. Oenophiles can indulge in a cheese and wine pairing at this cool speciality shop, which shines a light on lesser-known bottles by local small-scale producers.

La Casa del Tigre. See page 39. Fine dining with a playful twist; well, what else would you expect from a restaurant in a building whose former owner was rumoured to own a pet tiger?

Freskura. See page 69. Walk north to Alameda de Hércules and pause for a cone at this popular Italian-style gelato shop. Pistachio and *bacio* (chocolate and hazelnut) are two of their best flavours, but be on the lookout for seasonal fruit sorbets like fig or strawberry.

Churros and chocolate: a winning combo

Freiduría Puerta de la Carne

La Casa del Tigre

Off-grid Seville

Escape the crowds and head off the tourist trail to these lesser-known spots, from independent art galleries to beautifully conserved Baroque churches.

Art galleries in Alfalfa. See page 32. Alfalfa may be a tourist enclave, but duck down narrow sidestreets shooting out from the Plaza Alfalfa to discover small, independent art galleries; don't miss Berlin Galería, Más Cara Que Espalda and Delimbo.

Iglesia Omnium Sanctorum. See page 67. Easy to pass by among the local hustle and bustle of Calle Feria, the Iglesia Omnium Sanctorum, built in 1248 in the Gothic Mudéjar style, is the oldest standing church in Seville.

Mercado de Feria. See page 69. Explore this local fresh food market, with its colourful fruit and vegetable stalls, fish splayed out like ocean treasures, and an exceptional cured meat and cheese booth.

Palacio de las Dueñas, Casa de Alba. See page 64. One of the city's lesser-frequented monuments, but just as grandiose and worth the visit. Explore the palatial mansion and marvel at the flora that inspired famous poet Antonio Machado.

Iglesia de San Luis de los Franceses. See page 67. Discover one of the best-conserved (and lesser-known) Baroque masterpieces in the city at this deconsecrated church.

La Muralla Almohade. See page 67. You'll find the largest remnant of the Moorish city walls next to La Basílica de la Macarena. Walk below the walls, either inside the city or outside along the grassy knoll, as you gaze over the tenth-century fortress.

Casa Macareno. See page 70. Tapas, *ultramarinos* (preserved seafood, cheese and meats) and *montaditos* (small sandwiches) are all on the menu at this fine haunt on the Plaza Pumarejo, a once-dilapidated square now livened up with a funkier crowd.

Iglesia Omnium Sanctorum

Palacio de las Dueñas

La Muralla Almohade

PLACES

Plaza de España canal

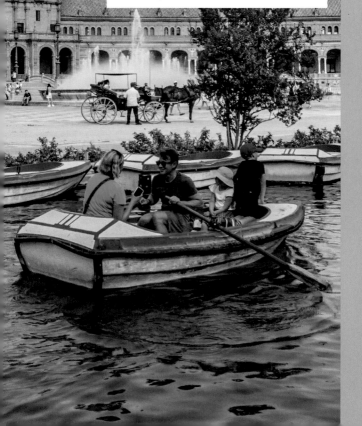

Centro Histórico

The Centro Histórico, or Historical Centre, stretches from Las Setas to Puerta Jerez and, despite being an easily walkable area, encompasses almost all of the Seville's big-hitting monuments: the Catedral, La Giralda and the Alcázar. In other words, it's where you're likely to spend most of your time. Here, you'll walk through, and literally on top of, almost 3000 years of history, from the Roman era to the resplendent Moorish period to Seville's illustrious Golden Age – at each corner, the lines between Moorish and Christian architecture blur beautifully. The main drag, Avenida de la Constitución, runs alongside the Catedral and is entirely pedestrianized, except for the tram that trundles from Plaza Nueva to a few other must-see spots south of the centre.

The Catedral

MAP PAGE 28, POCKET MAP E8
Avda. de la Constitución. www.catedralde
sevilla.es. Charge, combined Catedral and
Giralda tickets available; free Mon–Fri
2–3pm with reservation.

Seville's **Catedral** (properly titled Santa María de la Séde) was conceived in 1402 as an unrivalled monument to Christian glory – "a building on so magnificent a scale that posterity will believe we were mad". The canons, inspired by their vision of future repute, renounced all but a subsistence level of their incomes

The monumental tomb of Christopher Columbus in Seville's Catedral

to further enhance the building. The Catedral was completed in just over a century (1402–1506) – an extraordinary achievement, as it's the largest Gothic church in the world. As Norman Lewis says, "It expresses conquest and domination in architectural terms of sheer mass."

Though the church is built upon the huge, rectangular base-plan of the old mosque, the Christian architects (probably under the direction of the French master architect of Rouen cathedral) added the extra dimension of height. Its central nave rises to 42m, and even the side chapels seem tall enough to contain an ordinary church.

The *capilla mayor*, dominated by a vast Gothic *retablo* composed of forty-five carved scenes from the Life of Christ, is the lifetime's work of a single craftsman, Fleming Pieter Dancart. It is the Catedral's supreme masterpiece: the largest and richest altarpiece in the world and one of the finest examples of Gothic woodcarving. In the church's southeast corner, the Sacristía de los Cálices displays many of the Catedral's main art treasures, including a masterly image of *Santas Justa y Rufina* by Goya, depicting Seville's patron saints, who were executed by the Romans in 287.

To the left of the Sacristía, in front of the Puerta del Príncipe is the monumental tomb of Christopher Columbus. In the northwest corner, the Capilla de San Antonio has Murillo's *Vision of St Anthony* depicting the saint in ecstatic pose before an infant Christ. A magnificent artwork: see if you can spot where the restorers joined San Antonio back into place after he had been hacked out of the picture by thieves back in the nineteenth century. He was eventually discovered in New York – where savvy art dealers recognized the work they were

La Giralda offers fine city views

being asked to buy – and then returned to the Catedral.

La Giralda

MAP PAGE 28, POCKET MAP E8
Avda. de la Constitución. www.catedral desevilla.es. Charge, joint Giralda and Catedral tickets available; free Mon–Fri 2–3pm with reservation.

The entrance to **La Giralda** lies to the left of the Capilla Real in the Catedral's northeast corner. The cathedral's square-sided tower was named after the sixteenth-century *giraldillo*, or weather vane, on its summit, and it dominates the city skyline. You can climb to the bell chamber for a remarkable view of the city – and, equally remarkable, a glimpse of the Gothic details of the Catedral's buttresses and statuary. But most impressive of all is the tower's inner construction, a series of thirty-five gently inclined ramps wide enough to allow two mounted guards to pass.

The Giralda tower, before it was embellished with Christian additions, was the mosque's minaret and the artistic pinnacle of Almohad architecture. The Moorish structure took twelve

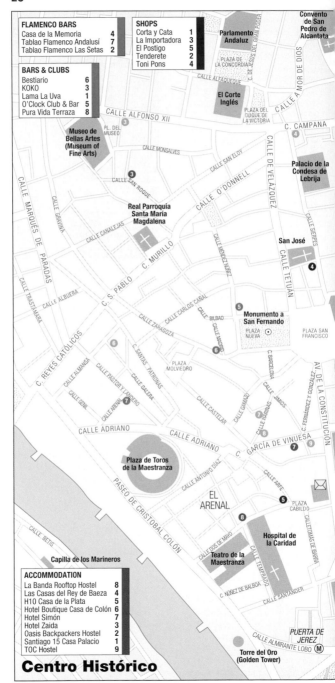

FLAMENCO BARS

Casa de la Memoria	4
Tablao Flamenco Andalusí	7
Tablao Flamenco Las Setas	2

BARS & CLUBS

Bestiario	6
KOKO	3
Lama La Uva	1
O'Clock Club & Bar	5
Pura Vida Terraza	8

SHOPS

Corta y Cata	1
La Importadora	3
El Postigo	5
Tenderete	2
Toni Pons	4

ACCOMMODATION

La Banda Rooftop Hostel	8
Las Casas del Rey de Baeza	4
H10 Casa de la Plata	5
Hotel Boutique Casa de Colón	6
Hotel Simón	7
Hotel Zaida	3
Oasis Backpackers Hostel	2
Santiago 15 Casa Palacio	1
TOC Hostel	9

Centro Histórico

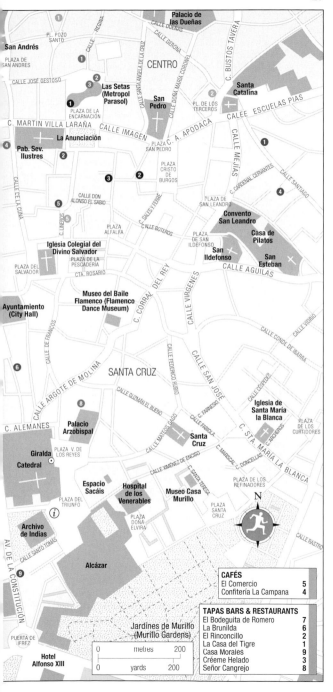

San Andrés
PL. POZO SANTO
PLAZA DE SAN ANDRES
CALLE JOSÉ GESTOSO
C. MARTIN VILLA LARAÑA
Pab. Sev. Ilustres
CALLE DE LA CUNA
C. LINEROS
CALLE DON ALONSO EL SABIO
Iglesia Colegial del Divino Salvador
PLAZA DEL SALVADOR
PLAZA DE LA PESCADERÍA
CTA. ROSARIO
Ayuntamiento (City Hall)
CALLE DE FRANCOS
C. ALEMANES
Giralda
Catedral
PLAZA V. DE LOS REYES
Espacio Sacáis
Archivo de Indias
CALLE SANTO TOMÁS
AV. DE LA CONSTITUCIÓN
PUERTA DE JEREZ
Hotel Alfonso XIII
Alcázar
PLAZA DEL TRIUNFO
Hospital de los Venerables
PLAZA DOÑA ELVIRA
Museo Casa Murillo
PLAZA DE LOS REFINADORES
PLAZA SANTA CRUZ
Santa Cruz
Palacio Arzobispal
CALLE ARGOTE DE MOLINA
CALLE GUZMÁN EL BUENO
SANTA CRUZ
CALLE FEDERICO RUBIO
C. CORRAL DEL REY
Museo del Baile Flamenco (Flamenco Dance Museum)
La Anunciación
CENTRO
Palacio de las Dueñas
CALLE DUEÑAS
CALLE GERONA
C. BUSTOS TAVERA
Santa Catalina
CALEE ESCUELAS PIAS
San Pedro
Las Setas (Metropol Parasol)
PLAZA DE LA ENCARNACIÓN
CALLE IMAGEN
PLAZA SAN PEDRO
PLAZA C. A. APODACA
PLAZA CRISTO DE BURGOS
C. SALES Y FERRE
C. CALLE BOTEROS
PLAZA ALFALFA
PLAZA DE SAN LEANDRO
Convento San Leandro
PLAZA DE SAN ILDEFONSO
San Ildefonso
Casa de Pilatos
San Esteban
CALLE AGUILAS
CALLE MEJÍAS
CALLE CARDENAL CERVANTES
CALLE SANTIAGO
CALLE VIRGENES
CALLE SAN JOSÉ
CALLE CONDE DE IBARRA
CALLE VIDRIO
C. CESPEDE
Iglesia de Santa María la Blanca
PLAZA DE LOS CURTIDORES
C. ARCHEROS
C. STA. MARÍA LA BLANCA
C. DONCELLAS
C. MARISCAL
CALLE XIMÉNEZ DE ENCISO
C. SANTA TERESA
CALLE RASTRO
N
CALLE DONA MARÍA CORONEL
CALLE SANTA ÁNGELA DE LA CRUZ
Jardines de Murillo (Murillo Gardens)

0   metres   200
0   yards   200

CAFÉS	
El Comercio	5
Confitería La Campana	4

TAPAS BARS & RESTAURANTS	
El Bodeguita de Romero	7
La Brunilda	6
El Rinconcillo	2
La Casa del Tigre	1
Casa Morales	9
Créeme Helado	3
Señor Cangrejo	8

years to build (1184–96) and derives its firm, simple beauty from the shadows formed by blocks of brick trelliswork (a style known as *sebka*), different on each side, and relieved by a succession of arched niches and windows. It was used by the Moors both for calling the faithful to prayer and as an observatory, and was so venerated that they wanted to destroy it before the Christian conquest of the city. This they were prevented from doing by the threat of Alfonso (later King Alfonso X) that "if they removed a single stone, they would all be put to the sword". Instead, it became the bell tower of the Christian Catedral. The original harmony has been somewhat spoiled by the Renaissance-era additions, but it remains one of the most important and beautiful monuments of the Islamic world.

Archivo de Indias

MAP PAGE 28, POCKET MAP E8
Avda. de la Constitución. Free.

If you have a keen interest in the Spanish Empire's travels to the Americas and Asia, visit the

Moorish Seville

Seville was one of the earliest Moorish conquests (in 712) and, as part of the Caliphate of Córdoba, became the second city of al-Andalus. When the caliphate broke up in the early eleventh century, it was by far the most powerful of the independent states (or *taifas*) to emerge, extending its power over the Algarve and eventually over Jaén, Murcia and Córdoba itself. This period, under a series of three Arabic rulers from the Abbadid dynasty (1023–91), was something of a golden age. The city's court was unrivalled in wealth and luxury and was sophisticated, too, developing a strong chivalric element and a flair for poetry – one of the most skilled exponents being the last ruler, al-Mu'tamid, the "poet-king". But with sophistication came decadence, and in 1091 Abbadid rule was overthrown by a new force, the Almoravids, a group of fanatical Amazigh Muslims from North Africa, to whom the Andalusians had appealed for help against the rising threat from the northern Christian kingdoms.

Despite initial military successes, the Almoravids failed to consolidate their gains in al-Andalus and attempted to rule through military governors from Marrakesh. In the middle of the twelfth century, they were in turn supplanted by a new Amazigh incursion, the Almohads, who by about 1170 had recaptured virtually all the former territories. Seville had accepted Almohad rule in 1147 and became the capital of this last real empire of the Moors in Spain. Almohad power was sustained until their disastrous defeat in 1212 by the combined Christian armies of the north, at Las Navas de Tolosa. In this brief and precarious period, Seville underwent a renaissance of public building, characterized by a new vigour and fluidity of style. The Almohads rebuilt the Alcázar, enlarged the principal mosque – later demolished to make room for the Christian Catedral – and erected a new and brilliant minaret, a tower over 100m tall, topped with four copper spheres that could be seen for miles around: La Giralda.

The Archivo de Indias shelters a mountain of historic documentation

sixteenth-century **Archivo de Indias** (General Archive of the Indies) between the Catedral and the Alcázar. Originally called La Casa Lonja, it served as the city's old stock exchange (*lonja*). Built in the severe and uncompromising style of El Escorial near Madrid, and designed by the same architect, Juan de Herrera, in the eighteenth century it was turned into a storehouse for the archive of the Spanish empire – a purpose it served for almost three hundred years.

In 2006, this mountain of documentation (of vital importance to scholars) was moved to another building around the corner and the UNESCO-protected Archivo was renovated, enabling visitors to enjoy Herrera's masterpiece in all its splendour once again.

Inside, the sumptuous marble floors, bookcases in Cuban wood, arcaded central patio, and grand staircase in pink and black marble are a visual feast. The upper floor houses temporary exhibitions of interesting documents plucked from the archive; these frequently include items such as Columbus's logbook and a letter from a penurious Cervantes (pre-*Don Quixote*) petitioning the king for a position in the Americas – fortunately for world literature, he was turned down.

The magnificent interior of the Alcázar

The Ayuntamiento

MAP PAGE 28, POCKET MAP E7

Pza. de San Francisco. 955 010 010.

Charge; free on Saturday with reservation.

Another building worth a visit and sited slightly to the north of the Catedral is the sixteenth-century **Ayuntamiento** (City Hall), which has a richly ornamented Plateresque facade by Diego de Riaño. The equally impressive interior of what's known as the Casa Consistorial – with Riaño's star-vaulted entrance hall and council chamber with gilded coffered ceiling – is open for guided visits. If you're lucky, you may even see a newlywed couple waltz out after celebrating their civil ceremony.

The Alcázar

MAP PAGE 28, POCKET MAP E8–9

www.alcazarsevilla.org. Charge; book tickets in advance to avoid long queues and arrive 15mins early.

Rulers of Seville have occupied the site of the **Alcázar** from the time of the Romans. Here was built the great court of the Abbadids, which reached a peak of sophistication and exaggerated sensuality under the ruthless al-Mu'tadid – a ruler who enlarged the palace to house a harem of eight hundred women, and who decorated the terraces with flowers planted in the skulls of his decapitated enemies. Later, under the Almohads, the complex was turned into a citadel, forming the heart of the town's fortifications. Its extent was enormous, stretching to the Torre del Oro.

Follow the art trail to Alfalfa

The area around Alfalfa's buzzing plaza, occasionally referred to as the Soho of Seville, is sprinkled with hidden art galleries and unexpected creative spaces. On Calle Don Alonso el Sabio, at number 8, is the studio and gallery of contemporary artist Jaime Abaurre, housed in Más Cara Que Espalda (www.mascaraqueespalda.com), a building designed by the same architect behind the Plaza de España. Here, Abaurre showcases his minimalist Pop Art drawings, from black and white line works to brightly coloured post-Impressionist designs. In a larger space down the street, Delimbo (www.delimbo.com), at Calle Pérez Galdós 1, features rotating collections of modern art, from paintings to sculptures to larger-scale installations. Tucked down a narrow sidestreet, the intimate Berlín Galería (C/Boteros 4; www.berlingaleria.es) is the brainchild of Jesús Barrera and highlights both emerging and established artists, each with their own distinct style expressed in a variety of mediums. Exhibitions at Berlín rotate every month and a half – if you happen to stumble upon an opening night, the party will be in full swing.

Parts of the Almohad walls survive, but the present structure of the palace dates almost entirely from the Christian period. Seville was a favoured residence of the Spanish kings for some four centuries after the Reconquest – most particularly of Pedro the Cruel (Pedro I; 1350–69) who, with his mistress María de Padilla, lived in and ruled from the Alcázar. Pedro's rebuild of the palace forms the nucleus of the Alcázar as it is today and, despite numerous restorations necessitated by fires and earth tremors, it offers some of the best surviving examples of Mudéjar architecture – the style developed by Moors working under Christian rule.

Later monarchs, however, have left all too many traces and additions. Isabel built a new wing in which to organize expeditions to the Americas and control the new territories; Carlos V married a Portuguese princess in the palace, adding huge apartments for the occasion; and under Felipe IV (c.1624) extensive renovations were carried out to the existing rooms.

In the beautiful and rambling **Jardines de los Reales Alcázares**, you'll find the vaulted baths in which María de Padilla is supposed to have bathed (in reality, an auxiliary water supply for the palace), and the Estanque de Mercurio with a bronze figure of the messenger of the gods at its centre. This Mercury Pond was specially built for Felipe V in 1733, who whiled away two solitary years at the Alcázar fishing and preparing himself for death through religious flagellation. South of here towards the centre of the gardens, there's an entertaining maze of myrtle bushes and, nearby, the pavilion (*pabellón*) of Carlos V, the only survivor of several he built for relaxation.

Plaza de la Encarnación and Las Setas

MAP PAGE 28, POCKET MAP E5-6
www.setasdesevilla.com.
Charge for mirador and museum.
Almost at the geographical centre of the former walled city of Seville, the **Plaza de la Encarnación** was created in 1819 after Napoleon's invading forces demolished the

Las Setas is a series of wood-waffle mushroom structures

convent of the same name that stood on the spot. Long criticized for its bleakness, at the start of the new millennium the city government decided to shake up its image with a breathtaking piece of modern architecture.

Taking seven years to build, **Las Setas**, or Metropol Parasol (as it is officially dubbed), is a 30m-high, 150m-long structure comprising a series of undulating wood-waffle flat-topped mushroom structures on giant concrete pillars. Claimed by its German architect, Jürgen Mayer, to be the world's largest timber construction, it incorporates a bustling food market, restaurants, bars and a basement museum that imaginatively displays the ruins of Roman Sevilla – complete with mosaics – encountered during the preliminary excavations. The structure's high point (in all senses) is a spectacular walkway across the roof to a sky deck with stunning views over the city.

When unveiled in 2011, the design attracted much criticism and its official name did not last more than a couple of days – *sevillano* residents took one look and tagged

it Las Setas ("The Mushrooms"), the name everyone uses today.

Palacio de la Condesa de Lebrija

MAP PAGE 28, POCKET MAP D6
C/Cuna 8. www.palaciodelebrija.com.
Charge.

The family home of the late Countess of Lebrija, this sixteenth-century **mansion** is arranged around a dazzling courtyard mixing Roman mosaics sourced from Itálica (see page 72), Mudéjar arches and Renaissance stonework. Inside, Roman glassware, ancient coins, and marble from Medina Azahara (see page 94) are among the treasures on display. On the first floor, a series of rooms is decorated in Baroque and Arabic styles, and includes a library filled with books on antiquity and a gallery of world-class contemporary art (guided tour only; included in ticket price).

Hospital de la Caridad

MAP PAGE 28, POCKET MAP D8
C/Temprado 3.
www.santa-caridad.es. Charge.
The **Hospital de la Caridad** was founded in 1676 by Don Miguel

The library, Palacio de la Condesa de Lebrija

Museo de Bellas Artes, one of Spain's finest art galleries

de Mañara, the inspiration for Byron's *Don Juan*. According to one of Don Miguel's friends, "There was no folly which he did not commit, no youthful indulgence into which he did not plunge … (until) what occurred to him in the street of the coffin." What occurred was that Don Miguel, returning from a reckless orgy, had a vision in which he was confronted by a funeral procession carrying his own corpse. He repented his past life, joined the Brotherhood of Charity (whose task was to bury the bodies of vagrants and criminals), and later set up this hospital for the relief of the dying and destitute, for which purpose it is still used.

Don Miguel commissioned a series of eleven paintings by Murillo for the chapel; seven remain (the French stole the others during the Napoleonic occupation), including a superlative image of *San Juan de Dios* for which Mañara himself posed as the model. Alongside hang two *Triumph of Death* pictures by Valdés Leal. One, depicting a decomposing bishop being eaten by worms (beneath the scales of justice labelled *Ni más, Ni menos* – No More, No Less), is so powerfully repulsive that Murillo declared that "you have to hold your nose to look at it". Their mood may reflect memories of the 1649 plague, which killed half of Seville's population.

Museo de Bellas Artes

MAP PAGE 28, POCKET MAP C6
Pza. del Museo 9.
www.museosdeandalucia.es.
Charge; free with EU passport.

Tucked into a shaded little plaza near the Plaza de Armas bus station is one of Spain's most impressive art galleries, the **Museo de Bellas Artes** (Museum of Fine Arts), housed in a beautiful former convent. The building itself, with its grand entrance and frescoed domed ceilings, is worth a visit, regardless of your interest in Baroque paintings.

While the collection of Spanish and *sevillano* artists features works throughout the fifteenth and twentieth century, the museum's focus is on the city's seventeenth-century Golden Age. Currently, the most emblematic room is beyond

Iglesia Colegial del Divino Salvador

a serene patio and cloister, in the monastery's former church. Along with works from Seville's important Baroque painters like Herrera del Viejo and Roelas, the nucleus of the collection is Zurbarán's *Apotheosis of St Thomas Aquinas*, as well as a clutch of works by Murillo in the apse, crowned by the great *Immaculate Conception* – known as "*La Colosal*" to distinguish it from the other work here with the same name. Below is the same artist's *Virgin and Child*; popularly known as *La Servilleta* because it was said to have been painted on a dinner napkin; the work is one of Murillo's greatest. Don't miss other important works like El Greco's portrait of his only son, *Retrato de Jorge Manuel Theotocópuli*, as well Murillo's *Santa Justa y Rufina*, depicting two venerated patron saints of Seville. Keep in mind that the collection is frequently rotated, so not all the works mentioned may be on show.

Every Sunday morning, over forty artists exhibit their works, from paintings to sculpture and photography, in the Plaza del Museo as part of a local art market.

Iglesia Colegial del Divino Salvador

MAP PAGE 28, POCKET MAP E6-7
Pza. del Salvador 3. www.catedralde
sevilla.es/iglesia-de-el-salvador. Charge,
entrance included in Catedral ticket.
Before hitting the ranks as the second largest church in Seville after the cathedral, **Iglesia Colegial del Divino Salvador** served as a Roman temple and, later in the eleventh century, as the city's main mosque. Evidence of its former role can be seen in both the Patio of Ablutions and its minaret-turned-bell tower. Today, the church is one of the impressive examples of seventeenth-century Baroque architecture in the city and it houses well-known paintings by the likes of Juan de Mesa and Juan Martínez Montañés.

Plaza de Toros de la Maestranza

MAP PAGE 28, POCKET MAP C8
C/Adriano 37. www.visitplazadetorosde
sevilla.com. Charge.
Seville's bullfighting ring – the **Plaza de Toros de la Maestranza** – serves two purposes. One is the actual bullfighting itself, while the other is the cultural and historical museum on the ground floor. Bullfights run from April through June and start up again for a few weekends in September and October (check www.plazadetorosdelamaestranza. com for dates). Whatever your stance on the ethical implications of bullfighting, it is undeniable that the spectacle is etched into the fabric of the city. A museum ticket allows you to walk through the bullring, which was built between 1761 and 1881 and can hold a staggering 12,500 spectators, and to visit various exhibits in which you'll gain an understanding of the deep-rooted history of the tradition and see a collection of dazzling costumes, posters and art by painters like Goya.

Shops

Corta y Cata

MAP PAGE 28, POCKET MAP E5
Pza. de la Encarnación, Puesto 10.
www.cortaycata.com.

At this gourmet food stall in the Mercado de Encarnación, owner Gema Alastuey brings in top-notch *jamon ibérico* from her hometown in Huelva, a neighbouring region known for producing some of the best cured pork in the world. You can stop by for a tasting in the morning or go for a full-on Iberian shopping spree (recommended), loading up on freshly cut packs of ham, chorizo and a plethora of other unique cured meats you've likely never heard of. Don't miss the local and national cheese selections as well.

La Importadora

MAP PAGE 28, POCKET MAP E6
C/Pérez Galdós 2. 954 561 829.

Concept store selling locally made clothes, jewellery, bags, homewares and spectacular artwork, much of which is painted by the owner, Rafael García Forcada.

Corta y Cata, Mercado de Encarnación

El Postigo

MAP PAGE 28, POCKET MAP D8
Lonja de Artesania El Postigo, C/Arfe s/n.
Mon–Fri 10am–7pm, Sat & Sun until 8pm.

Close to the Catedral, El Postigo is a local market showcasing the works of artists and craftspeople. Twenty artisanal workshops supply the market with everything from handmade jewellery and leatherworks to textiles, traditional ceramics and *azulejos*. Don't let the austere building put you off: behind its severe facade lies a light and airy gallery-like space.

Tenderete

MAP PAGE 28, POCKET MAP E6
C/García de Vinuesa 27. 654 639 368.

This unassuming corner shop sells handmade arts and crafts and local pottery. It has a particularly excellent offering of straw bags, mats and other interiors and lifestyle goods that are quintessentially Andalusian. A scattering of reclaimed furniture and vintage one-off homewares keeps buyers on their toes: no two visits are the same. Look out also for the glassware made locally in Seville's old glass factory.

The ornate interiors of *Confitería La Campana*

Toni Pons

MAP PAGE 28, POCKET MAP D6
C/Sierpes 66. www.tonipons.com.
With a couple of locations in the centre of town, this is the place to go to pick up a pair of traditional Spanish espadrilles; you'll find them here in practically every colour and style imaginable.

Cafés

El Comercio

MAP PAGE 28, POCKET MAP E6
C/Lineros 9.
Breakfast starts here with the city's best churros dunked into a steaming mug of hot chocolate, or perhaps with the venerated local breakfast toast drizzled with olive oil and topped with sliced tomato and cured ham. Wash it down with a robust *café con leche*. Founded in 1904, this family-run haunt has built up a loyal following, many of whom can be found propping up the original wooden bar counter. It's a charismatic space, with checkerboard tiles, glass-fronted cabinets and acres of wood. Out the back, a more formal restaurant with marble-topped tables is the perfect spot for tapas. €

Confitería La Campana

MAP PAGE 28, POCKET MAP D6
C/Sierpes 1.
A local stalwart on the café scene, *Confitería La Campana* has been going strong for nearly one hundred and forty years. Master pastry chef Antonio Hernández Merino set up shop in 1885 and, today, the café is in its fourth generation. Linger over a cup of coffee and one of the freshly baked pastries, either in the historic interior – all checkerboard flooring and ornate ceilings – or outside at one of the pavement tables. €

Tapas bars and restaurants

El Bodeguita de Romero

MAP PAGE 28, POCKET MAP D7
C/Harinas 10. 954 229 556.
With a few locations in the Arenal district of the city centre, this traditional *sevillano* bar dishes up plates of simple, classic tapas, like

the hearty pork-laden *montadito de pringá* sandwich. €

La Brunilda

MAP PAGE 28, POCKET MAP C7
C/Galera 5. www.labrunildatapas.com.
Husband-and-wife team chef Diego Caminos and oenologist Esperanza Nievas are behind this much-loved tapas bar. Traditional plates are given a contemporary twist, with that day's selection scrawled on the chalkboard menu. Set in a restored eighteenth-century coach house, this unpretentious haunt is a cosy spot – all exposed-brick walls and Bentwood chairs. Don't miss the crispy *buñuelos de bacalao* (cod fritters) served with pear aioli or the duck confit with spiced carrot purée. €€€

El Rinconcillo

MAP PAGE 28, POCKET MAP F5
C/Gerona 40. www.elrinconcillo.es.
Seville's oldest tapas bar has been serving up home-style dishes since 1670 and has stood the test of time. It's an utterly charming haunt. Walls are adorned with an eclectic mix of curios: hand-painted *azulejos* here, strings of cured

sausage there, a vintage telephone over there (a nod to its former life as a grocery store). Bills are totted up in chalk on the wooden bar counter. A more formal restaurant is upstairs. €€

La Casa del Tigre

MAP PAGE 28, POCKET MAP E5
C/Amparo 9. www.lacasadeltigre.com.
A fun fine-dining experience is inevitable in a building whose former owner was rumoured to own a pet tiger. Don't miss the mini brioche bites or its take on *patatas bravas*. €€€

Casa Morales

MAP PAGE 28, POCKET MAP D8
C/García de Vinuesa 11. 954 221 242.
Cosy up next to floor-to-ceiling clay wine barrels (which also serve as a chalkboard menu) in this fourth-generation tapas bar, just steps from the Catedral. €

Créeme Helado

MAP PAGE 28, POCKET MAP C6
Pza. del Museo 2.
www.facebook.com/creemehelado.
Make a little space for dessert with a walk to this ice-cream shop

El Rinconcillo, Seville's oldest tapas bar

on the Plaza del Museo where you'll find a bewildering selection of classic and creative flavours. The home-made concoctions are made from local, high-quality ingredients. The *mazapán* and the Plátano Warhol (banana, passion fruit, chocolate shavings) are some of the rotating stars here. €

Señor Cangrejo

MAP PAGE 28, POCKET MAP D8
C/Harinas 21. 955 092 910.
This inconspicuous but totally sleek concept pumps out perfectly executed takes on classic flavours from a shoebox-sized kitchen using exceptional products. The wine list is also noteworthy and leans towards natural and small-batch wineries. €€€

Bars and clubs

Bestiario

MAP PAGE 28, POCKET MAP D7
C/Zaragoza 33. 662 141 415.
A smaller DJ-fueled club with a wide age range of partygoers.

Pura Vida Terraza overlooks La Giralda

Head out on a Saturday and you may even catch a wedding party, bride and all, living it up into the small hours.

KOKO

MAP PAGE 28, POCKET MAP E5
Pza. de la Encarnación 38.
Hidden inside Las Setas, this lively hangout usually rocks a younger crowd and endless reggaeton music. Enjoy drinks at the surrounding neighbourhood bars beforehand and head inside when the crowd gets going.

Lama La Uva

MAP PAGE 28, POCKET MAP E5
C/Regina 1. www.lamalauva.com.
Practically in the shadow of Las Setas in Plaza de la Encarnación, this funky wine shop shines a light on local and lesser-known bottles. The brainchild of Cádiz-born Ana Linares, this cosy hangout is the ideal spot for a wine tasting paired with a cheese and charcuterie board. A handful of tables and chairs spill out onto the pavement outside and are the perfect perch for people-watching.

O'Clock Club & Bar

MAP PAGE 28, POCKET MAP D7
C/Méndez Núñez 17. 722 592 894.
Centrally located off Plaza Nueva and known for a well-heeled crowd that still knows how to get rowdy. Expect excellent gin and tonics and DJs playing Spanish music from decades past, with more reggaeton as the night goes on.

Pura Vida Terraza

MAP PAGE 28, POCKET MAP E7
Fontecruz Seises, C/Segovias 46.
www.puravidaterraza.com.
Seville has a plethora of rooftop bars, usually attached to hotels, but this one boasts some of the most coveted views of the luminous Giralda. With its relatively relaxed atmosphere and colourful cocktails, it's always a good time. Flamenco concerts are

Casa de la Memoria hosts nightly flamenco performances

hosted on Fridays and Saturdays so book a table in advance to catch the action. €

Flamenco bars

Casa de la Memoria
MAP PAGE 28, POCKET MAP E6
C/Cuna 6. www.casadelamemoria.es.
A cultural centre, museum and flamenco *tablao* in one, with a small exhibition space and string of vibrant courtyards. Founded in 1999, this long-running venue is housed in a fifteenth-century converted palace with bags of character. Soul-stirring flamenco performances are held nightly (except Monday) at 6pm and 7.30pm. If you walk by early enough, you may spot a dancer warming up for the show – pensively tapping and clapping at the entrance.

Tablao Flamenco Andalusí
MAP PAGE 28, POCKET MAP C7
C/Arenal 3.
www.tablaoflamencoandalusi.com.
This traditional standby in the Arenal neighbourhood hosts performances every day of the week at 6.30pm and 8.30pm. Seats are not assigned to tickets (which you should definitely buy in advance to avoid disappointment) so try to arrive as early as possible for the best views. Moving performances by talented dancers, singers and guitarists never fail to mesmerize the crowd in this intimate and atmospheric little venue.

Tablao Flamenco Las Setas
MAP PAGE 28, POCKET MAP E5
Setas de Sevilla, Pza. de la Encarnación.
www.tablaoflamencolassetas.com.
One of the newest and more modern *tablaos* in the city, located right in buzzy Las Setas, with nightly performances at 6pm and 8.30pm. A welcome drink is included in some tickets, and its extensive cocktail list boasts a gamut of creative sherry wine-infused libations. For the best seats in the house, you can upgrade your ticket to a guaranteed front-row spot or even inquire about flamenco classes if you feel inspired.

Santa Cruz

Stretching east from the Centro Histórico, Santa Cruz was the city's Jewish quarter until the Alhambra Decree of 1492. After a period of decline, the neighbourhood got back on its feet when wealth flooded into the city from trade with the Americas in the sixteenth century – the legacy of Spanish conquest can be seen in the fascinating Archivo de Indias. The scenic Plaza del Salvador stars in the work of Spanish writer Cervantes, including *Rinconete y Cortadillo*, in which he exposes the dark underbelly of the city during Spain's era of colonization. The *barrio* is very much in character with Seville's romantic image: its streets are narrow and tortuous to keep out the sun, its houses brilliantly whitewashed and festooned with flowering plants. The beauty of the quarter has inspired many a creative, most famously Spanish artist and *barrio* resident Murillo and Valdés Leal, who painted the Baroque frescoes splashed across the Hospital de los Venerables Sacerdotes. You only have to lose yourself in Santa Cruz's picturesque streets and stumble across hidden plazas, picturesque patios and handsome mansions to see why.

Whitewashed houses and cobbled alleys in Santa Cruz

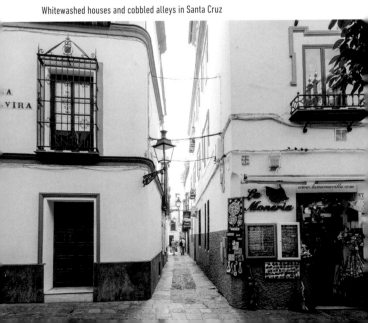

Casa de Pilatos

Casa de Pilatos

MAP PAGE 44, POCKET MAP F6
Pza. de Pilatos 1.
www.fundacionmedinaceli.org. Charge,
including audioguide; Mon 3–5pm free for
EU citizens with passport or ID card.

Of Santa Cruz's numerous
mansions, by far the finest is the
so-called **Casa de Pilatos**, built by
the Marqués de Tarifa on his return
from a pilgrimage to Jerusalem in
1519 and popularly thought to
have been in imitation of the house
of Pontius Pilate. In fact, it's an
interesting and harmonious mixture
of Mudéjar, Gothic and Renaissance
styles, featuring brilliant *azulejos*,
a tremendous sixteenth-century
stairway and one of the most elegant
domestic patios in the city. The
finest tilework adorns the staircase,
which is crowned by a gold-hued
artesonado dome; the first floor is
available to visit by guided tour. It
is still partly occupied by the ducal
Medinaceli family, whose portraits
span several centuries.

Hospital de los Venerables Sacerdotes

MAP PAGE 44, POCKET MAP E8
Pza. de los Venerables 8.
www.losvenerables.es.
Charge; Mon 3–6pm free.

Patios are a feature of almost all
the houses in Santa Cruz: they

Cultural riches

Santa Cruz is home to a thriving creative scene. Established
galleries like longstanding stalwart Rafael Ortiz (C/Mármoles
12; www.galeriarafaelortiz.com), housed in an eighteenth-
century palace, and Galería Haurie (C/Guzmán el Bueno 9;
www.galeriahaurie.com) have paved the way for a string of
emerging art hubs. Among these are Espacio Derivado (Pza.
Cristo de Burgos 17; www.espacioderivado.com), a cultural
centre hosting talks, exhibitions, film screenings, live music and
other events, and Espacio Sacáis (Pza. de la Alianza 3), a gallery
providing a platform for young artists from Andalucía.

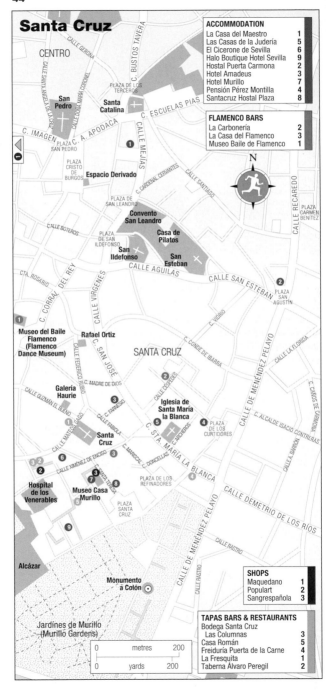

Santa Cruz

CENTRO

CALLE GERONA

C. BUSTOS TAVERA

CALLE SANTA ÁNGELA DE LA CRUZ

CALLE DOÑA MARÍA CORONEL

PLAZA DE LOS TERCEROS

San Pedro

Santa Catalina

C. ESCUELAS PIAS

C. IMAGEN

PLAZA SAN PEDRO

C. A. APODACA

CALLE MEJÍAS

PLAZA CRISTO DE BURGOS

Espacio Derivado

C. CARDENAL CERVANTES

CALLE SANTIAGO

CALLE RECAREDO

PLAZA CARMEN BENÍTEZ

PLAZA DE SAN LEANDRO

Convento San Leandro

CALLE BOTEROS

PLAZA DE SAN ILDEFONSO

Casa de Pilatos

San Ildefonso

San Esteban

CALLE AGUILAS

CALLE SAN ESTEBAN

PLAZA SAN AGUSTÍN

CTA. ROSARIO

C. CORRAL DEL REY

CALLE VIRGENES

C. VIDRIO

Museo del Baile Flamenco (Flamenco Dance Museum)

Rafael Ortiz

CALLE FEDERICO RUBIO

C. SAN JOSÉ

SANTA CRUZ

C. CONDE DE IBARRA

CALLE MENÉNDEZ PELAYO

CALLE LA FLORIDA

C. CARLOS DE CARMONA

Galería Haurie

C. MADRE DE DIOS

CALLE GUZMÁN EL BUENO

C. FARNESIO

C. FABIOLA

Iglesia de Santa María la Blanca

C. CÁCERES

C. ARCHEROS

PLAZA DE LOS CURTIDORES

CALLE ALCALDE ISACIO CONTRERAS

CALLE MATEOS GAGO

Santa Cruz

C. STA. MARÍA LA BLANCA

CALLE BARROM

C. MARISCAL

C. DONCELLAS

PLAZA DE LOS REFINADORES

CALLE BARROM

Hospital de los Venerables

C. XIMÉNEZ DE ENCISO

C. SANTA TERESA

Museo Casa Murillo

PLAZA SANTA CRUZ

CALLE DEMETRIO DE LOS RÍOS

Alcázar

Monumento a Colón

CALLE DE MENÉNDEZ PELAYO

CALLE RASTRO

CALLE RASTRO

Jardines de Murillo (Murillo Gardens)

	metres	200
0		
	yards	200
0		

N

ACCOMMODATION

La Casa del Maestro	1
Las Casas de la Judería	5
El Cicerone de Sevilla	6
Halo Boutique Hotel Sevilla	9
Hostal Puerta Carmona	2
Hotel Amadeus	3
Hotel Murillo	7
Pensión Pérez Montilla	4
Santacruz Hostal Plaza	8

FLAMENCO BARS

La Carbonería	2
La Casa del Flamenco	3
Museo Baile de Flamenco	1

SHOPS

Maquedano	1
Populart	2
Sangrespañola	3

TAPAS BARS & RESTAURANTS

Bodega Santa Cruz	
Las Columnas	3
Casa Román	5
Freiduría Puerta de la Carne	4
La Fresquita	1
Taberna Álvaro Peregil	2

are often surprisingly large and in summer they become the principal family living room. One of the most beautiful is within the **Hospital de los Venerables Sacerdotes**, a Baroque edifice near the centre in a plaza of the same name – one of the few buildings in the *barrio* worth actively seeking out. The former hospice also displays some outstanding artworks, including sculptures by Martínez Montañés and a painting of the *Last Supper* by Roelas, plus some wonderfully restored frescoes by Lucás Valdés and Valdés Leal, in addition to a *Fray Pedro de Oña* by Zurbarán displaying the artist's special gift for portraying white draperies. The Centro Velázquez displays works by the Spanish master, including a fine *Santa Rufina* and a spectacular *Inmaculada Concepción*.

Museo del Baile Flamenco

MAP PAGE 44, POCKET MAP E7
C/Manuel Rojas Marcos 3.
www.museoflamenco.com. Charge.
The **Museo del Baile Flamenco** (Flamenco Dance Museum) is an innovative and entertaining insight into the history and evolution of this emblematic *andaluz* art form. Set up in collaboration with celebrated flamenco dancer Cristina Hoyos, the museum is interactive (and multilingual), employing the latest sound and image technology to familiarize visitors with the origins of flamenco and the range of dance styles or "*palos*", which can all be seen at the touch of a button. The centre also stages flamenco shows, which bring the art form to life at a very high standard. A visit to the museum is also included in the show price.

Iglesia de Santa María la Blanca

MAP PAGE 44, POCKET MAP F8
C/Santa Maria la Blanca 5.
www.santamarialablanca.com. Free.
Small and unassuming from the exterior, **Iglesia de Santa María la Blanca** is Santa Cruz's most emblematic church. From the eleventh to the thirteenth century, the structure served as a mosque during the Moorish period – its former role evident in the Patio of Ablutions. In 1248, as a result of the Christian reconquest of the city,

Iglesia de Santa María la Blanca

Jardínes de Murillo

Fernando III entrusted the mosque to the Jewish community, and it was converted into a synagogue. The synagogue endured over a century until the anti-Jewish sentiments forced practitioners out in 1391 and the building was converted once again, but this time into a Catholic church, as it remains today. While the entryway was built in the Gothic style, the interior is definitively Baroque, thanks to the hands of architect Sánchez Falconete. The ceiling's intricate white plasterwork sets it apart from the other Baroque-style churches in the city.

Plaza Doña Elvira

MAP PAGE 44, POCKET MAP E8
When the French invaded Seville in the nineteenth century, they were concerned about properly controlling the confusing labyrinth-like Santa Cruz. In an attempt to keep a better eye on the residents, they destroyed parts of the neighbourhood walls and created a string of central plazas – one of which was **Plaza Doña Elvira**. Fondly named by locals after the woman who ran a comedy theatre in the same spot, the plaza was updated in the regionalist design and architecture (geometric tiles, orange trees, a central fountain) in preparation for the 1929 World Expo. It remains a peaceful spot to escape the sun today, with tree-shaded cafés and bars.

Jardínes de Murillo

MAP PAGE 44, POCKET MAP E9-F8
Avda. Menéndez Pelayo. Free.
Many petitions were made to utilize part of the Alcázar's gardens throughout the nineteenth and twentieth century. While permission was granted, nothing ever really came of these requests until King Alfonso XIII gifted half of the gardens to the city for the 1929 World Expo, providing another public green space in the city. In 1915, the architect Juan Talavera designed the gardens as you see them today. Stretching from the Callejón de Agua to the Paseo de Catalina de Ribera, the **Jardínes de Murillo** are adorned with ornamental fountains, colourful tiled benches, octagonal roundabouts, and dense clouds of vegetation including monstrous ficus trees.

Shops

Maquedano

MAP PAGE 44, POCKET MAP D6
C/Sierpes 40. 954 564 771.

Founded in 1896, this traditional hat shop is rooted in time and place. A cool window display entices passers-by inside its doors, where everything from Rocío pilgrimage hats to Spanish berets beg to be tried on. A great spot to pick up a handcrafted souvenir.

Populart

MAP PAGE 44, POCKET MAP E8
Pje. de Vila 4. www.populartsevilla.com.

Small, family-run shop selling traditional pottery, antiques, handpainted ceramics and intricately decorated *azulejos*. An absolute treasure trove of rare gems collected by the owner since the 1970s. Better still, international shipping can be arranged.

Sangrespañola

MAP PAGE 44, POCKET MAP F8
C/Santa Teresa 4. 945 227 226.

Don't let the intense name ("Spanish blood") deter you. This little shop sells gorgeous local artisanal goods, from handbags to ceramics to paintings. Look for artwork from street artist Sarah Guldberg, whose watercolours inspired by the city's innumerable geometric tiles set her work apart from more traditional styles.

Tapas bars and restaurants

Bodega Santa Cruz Las Columnas

MAP PAGE 44, POCKET MAP E8
C/Rodrigo Caro. 954 218 618.

In a long row of touristy (but beautiful) restaurants you'll find

Hats galore at Maquedano

a few neighbourhood haunts where locals still pour out onto the streets, tapas in one hand, a cold beer the other. This is one of them. Don't miss the fried eggplant with molasses, a classic *sevillano* dish. €

Casa Román

MAP PAGE 44, POCKET MAP F8
Pza. Venerables 1.
www.casaromansevilla.com.
Snuggled into an idyllic orange tree-shaded plaza, *Casa Román* is a reliable traditional tapas bar among a sea of more touristed eateries. Founded in 1934 by Román Castro, it remains in the same family to this day and has gained a name for serving some of the best *adobo* (marinated fried fish) and *ibérico jamón* in town. Friendly, efficient service and a good selection of wines by the glass. Pick one of the wooden tables outside to watch everyday street life unfold before you, all against a backdrop of the Hospital de los Venerables. €€

Freiduría Puerta de la Carne

MAP PAGE 44, POCKET MAP F8
C/Puerta de la Carne 2.
www.freiduriapuertadelacarne.com.
Dating back to 1928, the oldest fry shop in Seville serves some of the city's freshest fried fish – an Andalusian speciality – at wallet-friendly prices. This casual eatery is a great pit stop for a leisurely, sun-soaked lunch on the outdoor dining terrace. A paper cone overflowing with piping-hot *boquerones en adobo* (marinated and fried anchovies) is worth any wait you may encounter. €

La Fresquita

MAP PAGE 44, POCKET MAP F8
C/Mateos Gagos 29. 954 226 010.
If you're looking to experience Seville's Semana Santa outside of Holy Week, look no further than *La Fresquita*. With walls hidden beneath religious photos, incense wafting across the bar and videos of previous processions on

Bodega Santa Cruz Las Columnas

repeat, this dinky drinking den brings the festival spirit to you as you sip on your ice-cold beer. You'll be in good company: it's a favourite haunt of locals, who spill outside onto the pavement and the terrace across the road. The food is simple and delicious; think plates of charcuterie, cheese and *montaditos* (small sandwiches), and a handful of traditional stews like the *carne con tomate* (meat in tomato sauce). €

Taberna Álvaro Peregil

MAP PAGE 44, POCKET MAP E8
C/Mateos Gagos 22.
Owned by Álvaro Peregil (son of the late flamenco singer Pepe Peregil), this local watering hole up the street from *Las Columnas* (see page 47) is comprised of a pair of adjoining tile-adorned bars. Patrons crowd around the original mahogany bar counter, knocking back glasses of sherry. The fragrant *espinacas con garbanzos* (spinach with garbanzos) is a must-try, best washed down with the taberna's famous sweet wine made from fruit grown on the bitter orange trees lining the streets. €

Flamenco bars

La Carbonería

MAP PAGE 44, POCKET MAP F7
C/Céspedes 21.
Housed in a converted coal factory, this flamenco bar is undeniably touristy thanks to its free entry but it still manages to retain its local charm despite the relentless crowds. Performances are loosely scheduled throughout the evening and simultaneously spontaneous. Arrive early to be first in the queue when doors open at 7pm to guarantee a good seat for the first show. Also hosts art exhibitions, poetry readings, literary events, film screenings, painting sessions and other cultural events.

Museo Baile de Flamenco

La Casa del Flamenco

MAP PAGE 44, POCKET MAP F8
C/Ximénez de Enciso 28.
www.lacasadelflamencosevilla.com.
No mics here at this pint-sized *tablao*, as the acoustics let these top-level performers' voices, instruments and *taconeos* speak for themselves. Shows generally run at 5.30pm, 7pm, 8.30pm and 10pm, with variations in schedule depending on the day and season (check online for up-to-date performance times).

Museo Baile de Flamenco

MAP PAGE 44, POCKET MAP E7
C/Manuel Rojas Marcos 3.
www.museoflamenco.com.
Apart from exhibitions, the museum also stages live performances featuring stars from the Cristina Hoyos flamenco school. Shows usually at 5pm, 7pm and 8.45pm. Buy the combined show and museum ticket and arrive half-hour early for a quick browse before the main event.

Sur

South of the Alcázar is Sur, the southern area of the city, which also encompasses the neighbourhoods of El Prado de San Sebastián and San Bernardo. While it could technically fit right into the Centro Histórico, the amplified avenues give the feeling you're far from the winding alleyways of downtown Seville. The enclosed gardens and green spaces provide natural respite and unprecedented tranquility, yet the most important sight here by far is the Plaza de España, which sits across from the Parque de María Luisa and wraps visitors within its majestic half-moon embrace. Get your culture hit at the Museum of Popular Arts and Traditions and La Fundación Valentín de Madariaga y Oya, home to a curated collection of contemporary art by Spanish painters.

Antigua Fábrica de Tabacos (Royal Tobacco Factory)

MAP PAGE 52, POCKET MAP F10
C/San Fernando 4. 954 551 048.
Free, by appointment only.

Immediately south of the Alcázar and fronting Avenida San Fernando lies the old tobacco factory and the setting for Bizet's *Carmen*. Now part of the University of Seville, the massive **Antigua Fábrica de Tabacos** was built in the 1750s and, in its heyday, contributed to Seville's phenomenal wealth

Parque de María Luisa, the green lung of Seville

Plaza de España

from a monopoly on trade with America. At its peak in the 1800s, it was the country's largest single employer. The factory packed in a workforce of some four thousand women, *cigarreras*, who made the cigars and cigarettes by hand. Many of the employees were Roma from the Triana neighbourhood – the inspiration for Bizet's fiery tragic heroine *Carmen*. Free tours, usually on weekday mornings, can be booked in advance.

Parque de María Luisa

MAP PAGE 52, POCKET MAP F12
Paseo de las Delicias.

A ten-minute walk south of the Alcázar lies the **Parque de María Luisa**, a wonderfully relaxing place to escape the city bustle and among the most pleasant public parks in Spain. It used to be wrapped up in the vast grounds of the Palacio de San Telmo but the palace's nineteenth-century owner, the dowager duchess María Luisa, donated the park to the city in 1893, which then named it after her. Bursting with flora and fauna, it's the perfect spot to escape the sweltering sun; take refuge in the shade of a ficus and watch the swans swim across the pond. Amid the ornamental pools and tree-shaded avenues lie various pavilions from the '29 Ibero-American Expo, and farther along at the southern end of the park is the Plaza de América, where you'll find a couple of airy cafés and children chasing the park's resident pigeons.

Plaza de España

MAP PAGE 52, POCKET MAP F11
Nudging up to the Parque de María Luisa is the **Plaza de España**, which was designed as the centrepiece of the 1929 Ibero-American Expo. A vast semicircular complex, with its fountains, monumental stairways and mass of tilework, it would seem strange in most Spanish cities, but here it looks entirely natural, carrying on the tradition of civic display. At the fair, the plaza was used for the Spanish exhibit of industry and crafts, and around the crescent are *azulejo* scenes representing each of the provinces – an

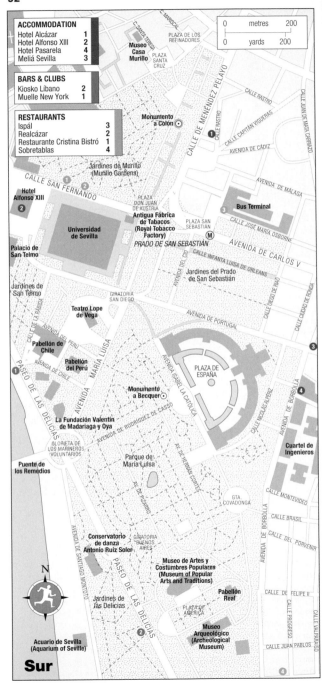

ACCOMMODATION
Hotel Alcázar	1
Hotel Alfonso XIII	2
Hotel Pasarela	4
Meliá Sevilla	3

BARS & CLUBS
Kiosko Líbano	2
Muelle New York	1

RESTAURANTS
Ispál	3
Realcázar	2
Restaurante Cristina Bistró	1
Sobretablas	4

Museo Casa Murillo

PLAZA DE LOS REFINADORES

C. MARISCAL

C. SANTA TERESA

PLAZA SANTA CRUZ

CALLE DE MENÉNDEZ PELAYO

CALLE RASTRO

CALLE JUAN DE MATA CARRIAZO

CALLE CAPITÁN VIGUERAS

Monumento a Colón

AVENIDA DE CÁDIZ

Jardines de Murillo (Murillo Gardens)

CALLE SAN FERNANDO

AVENIDA DE MÁLAGA

Hotel Alfonso XIII

PLAZA DON JUAN DE AUSTRIA

Antigua Fábrica de Tabacos (Royal Tobacco Factory)

PLAZA SAN SEBASTIÁN

Bus Terminal

CALLE JOSÉ MARÍA OSBORNE

Universidad de Sevilla

PRADO DE SAN SEBASTIÁN

AVENIDA DE CARLOS V

Palacio de San Telmo

AVENIDA DEL CID

CALLE INFANTA LUISA DE ORLEANS

Jardines de San Telmo

Jardines del Prado de San Sebastián

CALLE DIEGO DE RIAÑO

CALLE CIUDAD DE RONDA

GIRATORIA SAN DIEGO

Teatro Lope de Vega

CALLE DE LA RÁBIDA

AVENIDA DEL PERÚ

AVENIDA DE PORTUGAL

Pabellón de Chile

AVENIDA DE CHILE

AVENIDA MARÍA LUISA

PLAZA DE ESPAÑA

Pabellón del Perú

PASEO DE LAS DELICIAS

AVENIDA ISABEL LA CATÓLICA

AVENIDA DE BORBOLLA

Monumento a Becquer

La Fundación Valentín de Madariaga y Oya

AVENIDA DE RODRÍGUEZ DE CASSO

CALLE NICOLÁS ALPÉRIZ

Cuartel de Ingenieros

GLORIETA DE LOS MARINEROS VOLUNTARIOS

Parque de María Luisa

AV. DE HERNÁN CORTÉS

Puente de los Remedios

AV. DE PIZARRO

GTA. COVADONGA

CALLE MONTEVIDEO

CALLE BRASIL

AVENIDA DE SANTIAGO MONTOTO

GIRATORIA BUENOS AIRES

DE CALLE DEL PORVENIR

AVENIDA DE BORBOLLA

Conservatorio de danza Antonio Ruiz Soler

PASEO DE LAS DELICIAS

Museo de Artes y Costumbres Populares (Museum of Popular Arts and Traditions)

Pabellón Real

CALLE DE FELIPE II

Jardines de las Delicias

PLAZA DE AMÉRICA

CALLE PROGRESO

CALLE VALPARAÍSO

N

Acuario de Sevilla (Aquarium of Seville)

Museo Arqueológico (Archeological Museum)

CALLE JUAN PABLOS

Sur

metres 200

yards 200

0

0

Festival fever

Seville comes alive in spring when two huge festivals descend on the city. First up, Semana Santa, or Holy Week, is a highlight on the cultural calendar. In the week leading up to Easter, religious processions carting huge biblical statues (*pasos*) parade through the streets in homage to the Passion of Jesus Christ. Two weeks later, festival season reaches fever pitch as the Feria de Abril, or April Fair, takes over huge fairgrounds in Los Remedios, south of Triana. It's a week-long extravaganza of dance, music, food, drink, light displays, horse shows and daily bullfights. Festivities spill out of the fairground into Calle del Infierno and surrounding streets, with crowds clustering inside the 1000-plus striped *casetas* – marquee-style bars for drinking and dancing. Only a handful are open to the public: your best bets are Caseta Turística at C/Pascual Márquez 225; Área de Fiestas Mayores at C/Costillares 13; and La Marimorena at C/Manolo Vazquez 31. Each of Seville's seven city districts and its political parties and trade unions also have *casetas* that are open to tourists.

interesting record of the country at the tail end of a moneyed era. The buildings here fell into a terrible state in the latter part of the twentieth century but have now been superbly restored and refurbished. Today, many of the pavilions are used as museums, cultural centres, embassies, military headquarters and university buildings. The tiny strip of canal fronting the plaza has been refilled with water and folk can be seen once again pottering about in the little rented boats.

Museo de Artes y Costumbres Populares

MAP PAGE 52, POCKET MAP F13
Pabellón Mudéjar, Parque de María Luisa.
The **Museo de Artes y Costumbres Populares** (Museum of Popular Arts and Traditions) occupies one of the Ibero-American Expo pavilions, the stunning Pabellón Mudéjar. The collection itself is low-key, with exhibits including nineteenth-century costumes, antique glassware, ceramics, furniture, musical instruments and farm machinery.

A highlight is the replica artisanal workshops detailing age-old craft traditions like lacemaking, leatherwork and goldsmithing, and the exhibit of *azulejos*, many produced in Englishman Charles Pickman's factory in the Monastery of Cartuja.

Museo de Artes y Costumbres Populares

Acuario de Sevilla

La Fundación Valentín de Madariaga y Oya

MAP PAGE 52, POCKET MAP E11
Avda. María Luisa s/n. 954 366 072.
Right next to Parque de María Luisa, in one of the beautiful Expo 1929 pavilions, **La Fundación Valentín de Madariaga y Oya** houses a small curation of contemporary art from the twentieth century and twenty-first centuries. The permanent collection is themed around nature and the environment and features Spanish artists like Cristina Iglesias as well as global big-hitters like Andy Warhol and Joseph Beuys. Temporary exhibitions are also held here, showcasing a variety of different mediums from painting, sculpture and art installations to videos and photography.

Jardines de las Delicias and Líbano

MAP PAGE 52, POCKET MAP F13
Avda. de la Palmera
Across the street from Parque de María Luisa is a pair of connected gardens also worth exploring. The romantic **Jardines de las Delicias and Líbano** combine natural landscapes with quiet spaces, all crisscrossed by walking paths peppered with decorative fountains and marble busts from the Archbishop's Palace in neighbouring Umbrete. Tree-shaded cafés and bars are scattered around the parks, where you'll find locals sipping coffee or lingering over a late-night gin and tonic.

Acuario de Sevilla

MAP PAGE 52, POCKET MAP E13
Muelle de las Delicias.
www.acuariosevilla.es. Charge.
The installations at the **Acuario de Sevilla** (Aquarium of Seville), inspired by Ferdinand Magellan's exploration of the Pacific, include historical voyages displaying marine creatures in the Guadalquivir, Atlantic, Amazon, Pacific and Indo-Pacific. The aquarium houses about four hundred species in total. The most notable exhibit is the shark tank, which is the deepest in the Iberian Peninsula and accessed through a glass tunnel. Visitors can also reserve the entreMares dining experience to eat alongside its fanged sea creatures.

Restaurants

Ispál

MAP PAGE 52, POCKET MAP G9, G10
Pza. de San Sebastián 1.
www.restauranteispal.com.
Named after the original city
dating back to the eighth
century, *Ispál* focuses primarily
on the cuisine of Seville and its
neighbouring provinces, both in
recipe inspiration and ingredient
sourcing. The incense-perfumed
torrija (a Holy Week dessert
staple) is especially memorable.
€€€€

Realcázar

MAP PAGE 52, POCKET MAP E9, E10
C/San Fernando 27. www.realcazar.com.
Artfully presented Andalusian-
Mediterranean cuisine that looks
as good as it tastes. Meals are
served on an attractive plant-filled
terrace overlooking the Antigua
Fábrica de Tabacos. The speciality
is paella. €€€

Restaurante
Cristina Bistró

MAP PAGE 52, POCKET MAP E9
C/San Fernando 19. www.cristinabistro.es.
Right by the iconic *Alfonso
XIII* hotel, this contemporary
Andalusian tavern dishes up
traditional home-cooked cuisine
in a relaxed environment. A
smattering of outdoor tables
is the best spot for people-
watching. €€€

Sobretablas

MAP PAGE 52, POCKET MAP G13
C/Colombia 7.
www.sobretablasrestaurante.com.
Tucked a street behind the Plaza
de América, this award-winning
fine-dining restaurant redefines
Andalusian fare, served in a
bright and airy foliage-filled
space. The tasting menu, along
with its exceptional wine pairings
highlighting local varietals, is
highly recommended. €€€€

Bars and clubs

Kiosko Líbano

MAP PAGE 52, POCKET MAP F13
Paseo de las Delicias 151.
www.kioscolibano.com.
Nestled into the Jardines de
Delicias and Líbano, this bar is the
perfect spot for an afternoon pick-
me-up or alfresco nightcap. With
late-night DJs, the kiosk turns into
an outdoor club after hours.

Muelle New York

MAP PAGE 52, POCKET MAP E11
Paseo de las Delicias 3.
www.muellenewyork.es.
Somewhere between a bar and a
club, this forever-lively watering
hole along the Río Guadalquivir
hosts frequent live DJs in the
evenings on its riverside patio. Go
for an afternoon spritz or a late-
night mojito.

Outdoor tables at *Cristina Bistró*

Triana and the Río Guadalquivir

Down by the Río Guadalquivir, pedalboats putter along the waterway and locals sip beer on its banks. Very few people swim here, however, as the slow current means that it's more stagnant than a clean body of water. The main landmark is the twelve-sided Torre del Oro. Unfurling from the west bank of the Guadalquivir is Triana, a traditionally working-class *barrio* away from the heavily touristed trail. This was once the heart of the city's *gitano* community and, more specifically, home of the great flamenco dynasties of Seville who were kicked out by developers in the early twentieth century and are now scattered throughout the city. The *gitanos*, belonging to the Romani group, lived among extended families in tiny, immaculate communal houses called *corrales* built around courtyards glutted with flowers. Today, only a handful remain intact, best seen in Calle de Castilla and Calle Pagés del Corro. Triana is the starting point for the annual pilgrimage to El Rocío (end of May), when a myriad of oxen-drawn painted wagons leaves town. It is also home to the city's oldest working ceramics factory, Santa Ana, where the tiles, many still in the traditional, geometric Arabic designs, are hand-painted in the adjoining shop.

Torre del Oro, a landmark on the Río Guadalquivir

Puente de Isabel II, or Triana Bridge

Torre del Oro

MAP PAGE 58, POCKET MAP D9
Pza. de Cristóbal Colón. Charge.

Built by the Almohads in 1220 as part of the Alcázar fortifications, the **Torre del Oro** (Golden Tower) was connected to another small fort across the river by a chain that had to be broken by the Castilian fleet before their conquest of the city in 1248. On the banks of the Guadalquivir, the tower was later said to be used as a repository for the gold brought back from the Americas and also as a tax-collection point – hence the many legends swirling around its name.

Today, it's an iconic city landmark standing sentinel above the riverbank. A visit to the tower takes you through a maritime museum filled with navigation charts, models, compasses and ancient documents, and up to the rooftop viewing platform where you can look out over the river like a watchful Spanish vigilante.

Puente de Isabel II (Triana Bridge)

MAP PAGE 58, POCKET MAP B8

Officially named the **Puente de Isabel II**, this romantic nineteenth-century bridge straddling the Guadalquivir connects the city centre with the vibrant Triana neighbourhood. Construction began in 1845 and, seven years later, it became the

River cruises

River cruises depart from the Torre del Oro to discover a short stretch of the Guadalquivir that flows across Andalucía from the Sierra de Cazorla to the Gulf of Cádiz. It is the only navigable river in Spain. A boat ride offers views of Seville sights like the bullring, Puente de Isabel II, the Palacio de San Telmo and the Royal Tobacco Factory immortalized by Bizet's famous opera, *Carmen*. Other ways of traversing the water are by kayak, canoe and paddle board.

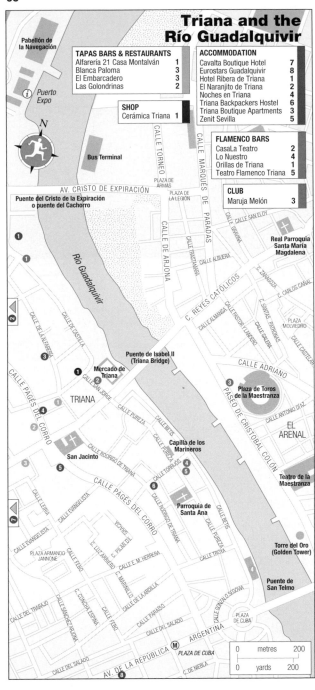

Triana and the Río Guadalquivir

TAPAS BARS & RESTAURANTS

Alfarería 21 Casa Montalván	1
Blanca Paloma	3
El Embarcadero	3
Las Golondrinas	2

SHOP

Cerámica Triana	1

ACCOMMODATION

Cavalta Boutique Hotel	7
Eurostars Guadalquivir	8
Hotel Ribera de Triana	1
El Naranjito de Triana	2
Noches en Triana	4
Triana Backpackers Hostel	6
Triana Boutique Apartments	3
Zenit Sevilla	5

FLAMENCO BARS

CasaLa Teatro	2
Lo Nuestro	4
Orillas de Triana	1
Teatro Flamenco Triana	5

CLUB

Maruja Melón	3

Flamenco

Flamenco developed as a way for the Roma to express the sadness and despair of their downtrodden lives. Triana, the historic Roma neighbourhood of Seville, is thought to be the birthplace of this soulful dance. For this reason, it's the best place to experience a traditional performance. Sometimes, there's no full-on show, just a singer and musician expressing a shared passion for music and movement – not necessarily any dancing. These intimate performances can be just as moving and mesmerizing as a theatrical display, if not more so. You won't find many bars that are more authentic than *CasaLa Teatro* (see page 63), an atmospheric 28-seat *tablao* in the Mercado de Triana. Other excellent flamenco bars in the city include the *Casa de la Memoria* (see page 41) and *La Carbonería* (see page 45). Museo Baile de Flamenco (see page 45) offers an excellent insight into the history of the tradition.

first solid bridge in Seville, having replaced a Moorish twelfth-century floating bridge made from pontoon boats.

From morning to night, locals lounge along the banks of the Guadalquivir beneath the metal arch, picnicking and enjoying the cooling river breeze. After dark, the bridge is prettily illuminated. To view the edifice from a different perspective, take a boat ride (see box, page 57) from the Torre del Oro or join a stand-up paddleboarding tour (www.paddlesurfsevilla.com) to glide beneath the oldest of Seville's decorative bridges.

The remains of Castillo de San Jorge

Mercado de Triana

Mercado de Triana and Castillo de San Jorge

MAP PAGE 58, POCKET MAP B8
C/San Jorge 6. Market: Mon–Sat 9am–3pm.
www.mercadodetrianasevilla.com.
Museum: temporarily closed. 955 470 255.

At the end of the Puente de Isabel II is **Mercado de Triana** and, on the floor beneath, the remains of the Castillo de San Jorge, which served as the seat of the infamous Spanish Inquisition from 1481 to 1785. In the early nineteenth century, the *castillo* was destroyed and a market built over its foundations. The ruins were rediscovered in 1990, and have been converted into a museum with chilling accounts of the Inquisition's unscrupulous goings-on and the history of the *castillo* (temporarily closed at the time of writing).

The central covered *mercado* is one of the best fresh food markets in the city and an ideal spot to pick up picnic supplies. Or stick around until lunch and pick from one of the many cheap-and-cheerful tapas bars and stalls. There's even a culinary school, Taller Andaluz de Cocina, right in the heart of the market which offers hands-on cookery classes using the freshest ingredients from the surrounding food stalls; it also runs guided market tours.

Capilla de los Marineros

MAP PAGE 58, POCKET MAP C8
C/Pureza 57. Chapel free,
charge for museum.

Dating back to 1759, the **Capilla de los Marineros** not only houses one of the most important Catholic brotherhoods in the city, but it also shelters a highly venerated depiction of the Virgin Mary, the Esperanza de Triana. During Holy Week, the statue is whisked out of the church and paraded through the streets for hours, accompanied by thousands of members of the brotherhood.

Outside Semana Santa, peek inside the church for an up-close view of the Virgin's elaborate embroidered dressings.

Pabellón de la Navegación

MAP PAGE 58, POCKET MAP A5
Camino de los Descubrimientos 2.
www.pabellondelanavegacion.com. Charge.

Another remnant of the World Expo '92, the **Pabellón de la Navegación** on the southern fringes of the Isla de la Cartuja has been turned into an exhibition space dedicated to the history of Spanish navigation and 'discovery'. With lots of interactive gadgetry and decent English translations, the museum is divided into four main sections: explorers, the history of navigation, shipboard life, and the role of Seville as a significant port with a monopoly on trade with America.

Kids will love the chance to reenact life aboard, stepping into the role of captain, sailor or cabin hand and taking charge of the rudder, sails or bilge pump to ensure safe sailing during a storm and under attack from corsairs.

Rich ceramics tradition

Triana was historically a creative enclave sheltering artisans, flamenco dancers and bullfighters. Today, a new generation is breathing life into the ancient tradition of ceramics, which has been practised in the *barrio* since the sixteenth century. A cluster of workshops can be found on and around Calle Antillano Campos, where you can peek at the artisans at work and buy ceramics. On Calle Callao, Cerámica Triana (see page 62) is a museum with exhibits tracing the production process and showcasing the artistry of the ceramicists.

Your entry ticket also allows you to climb the 65m-high Torre Schindler, taking its name from the Swiss company who built it, to a mirador offering stunning views over the Guadalquivir and the city.

La Cartuja and CAAC

MAP PAGE 58, POCKET MAP A3–4
www.caac.es. Charge, free Tues–Fri 7–9pm & Sat 11am–9pm with EU passport.

At Triana's northern edge lies **La Cartuja**, a fourteenth-century former Carthusian monastery expensively restored as part of the World Expo '92. Part of the complex is now given over to

the **Centro Andaluz de Arte Contemporáneo** (CAAC), which stages rotating exhibitions from a large and interesting collection of contemporary work by *andaluz* artists, including canvases by Antonio Rodríguez Luna, Joaquín Peinado, Guillermo Pérez Villalta, José Guerrero and Daniel Vásquez Díaz. Two galleries stage temporary exhibitions by cutting-edge international artists and photographers. In 2024/25, the CAAC is expected to move to the Reales Atarazanas in the Arenal neighbourhood; check the website for details.

Pabellón de la Navegación

Shop

Cerámica Triana

MAP PAGE 58, POCKET MAP B8
C/Callao 14. www.ceramicatriana.com.
Triana is known for its colourful
ceramics; pottery made from
riverside clay was once a primary
trade in the neighbourhood and
it continues to be a proud symbol
of local artistry. While there are
a few ceramics shops in the area,
Cerámica Triana has one of the
larger selections.

Tapas bars and restaurants

Alfarería 21 Casa Montalván

MAP PAGE 58, POCKET MAP B8
C/Alfarería 21.
www.facebook.com/alfarera21Triana.
From hidden stone enclaves to
rooftop perches with fine city
views, there isn't a bad seat in
the house at this emblematic
building, outfitted in vibrant
local design and architecture. The

Cerámica Triana

brainchild of brothers Paco, Pepe
and Carlos Arcas, this welcoming
hangout has a bar downstairs
and a restaurant above. Cuisine
is classic Spanish with a few
elevated twists. €€

Blanca Paloma

MAP PAGE 58, POCKET MAP A9
C/San Jacinto 49. 954 333 640.
Its name a colloquial nod to the
venerated Virgin of Triana, the
"White Dove" has a bustling
tapas bar on the ground floor
and a sit-down restaurant above.
Though you might have to wait
a while for a table, downstairs
is the best option for traditional
local plates at a much more
reasonable price. €

El Embarcadero

MAP PAGE 58, POCKET MAP D9
C/Betis 69B. 954 285 001.
A casual riverside bar and
restaurant with a large outdoor
dining terrace and straight-shot
views of the Torre del Oro. Keep
your eyes peeled for the discreet
ship door entrance, as it's easy to
miss. The kitchen specializes in
fish and seafood. €

Las Golondrinas

MAP PAGE 58, POCKET MAP A8
C/Antillano Campos 26. 954 331 626.
Decorated with traditional Triana
tiles, *Las Golondrinas* is a bustling
tapas bar with daily specials
like aioli-filled mushrooms and
garlicky carrots doused in olive oil.
There is a second location in the
neighbourhood but it's fun to stick
to the original.

Club

Maruja Melón

MAP PAGE 58, POCKET MAP C8
Paseo de Cristóbal Colón 11.
www.marujamelonsevilla.com.
One of the larger and better
cocktail bars, lounges and clubs on
Paseo de Cristóbal Colón, just a

The emblematic *Alfarería 21 Casa Montalván*

block from the river near the Triana Bridge and a hotspot for nightlife. There's a 1960s upscale bohemian vibe about the place, with areas for dancing and drinking inside, or lounging on the patio.

Flamenco bars

CasaLa Teatro
MAP PAGE 58, POCKET MAP B8
Pza. del Altozano, Mercado de Triana. www.casalateatro.com.
Flamenco is very much a part of daily life in Seville, and even more so in Triana. The mundane (grocery shopping) and the musical collide at this *tablao* located inside the Mercado de Triana. Delightfully intimate venue with only 28 seats. The daily show starts at 6pm; arrive early.

Lo Nuestro
MAP PAGE 58, POCKET MAP C8
C/Betis 31A.
A tiled plaque marks the unassuming entrance to this raucous bar, where live bands and flamenco dancers take to the stage. There's an extremely

fun atmosphere here, though as the best-known flamenco bar in Seville, it can get very crowded. Very welcoming; expect to be up and trying your hand at *sevillana* (traditional folk dance) before the night is out.

Orillas de Triana
MAP PAGE 58, POCKET MAP A7
C/Castilla 94. www.flamenqueria.es.
Not your typical *tablao*, this part dance school, part theatre is dedicated to the study of both traditional and evolving styles of flamenco. Experience the intensity and folklore while you take in serene views of the Río Guadalquivir through the floor-to-ceiling windows.

Teatro Flamenco Triana
MAP PAGE 58, POCKET MAP C9
C/Pureza 76. www.teatroflamencotriana.com.
This 100-seat theatre sets the stage for tremendously talented performers from Cristina Heeran's international flamenco school, recognized by the Ministry of Culture and the Andalusian Council. Shows run seven days a week at 7.30pm and 9pm.

Alameda, San Lorenzo and Macarena

The northern corner of Seville – from just behind Las Setas on Calle Feria up to the city walls along the Básicila de la Macarena – is home to the Alameda, San Lorenzo and Macarena neighbourhoods. Not long ago, La Alameda in particular was a downtrodden part of town to be avoided. Now, it has emerged as a hipster haven, with its funky vintage shops, fusion restaurants and popping late-night scene. On weekend nights, the bars are full to the brim with revellers while teens take over the Alameda de Hércules to engage in the youthful pastime of *botellón*, a Spanish tradition of drinking and socializing in the streets. San Lorenzo is a sleepier enclave to the west, sheltering hidden culinary gems and the locally venerated Jesús del Gran Poder. Macarena, to the north, is also home to an important basílica (after which it is named) along with towering remains of the ancient city walls.

Palacio de las Dueñas

MAP PAGE 66, POCKET MAP F5
C/Dueñas 5. www.lasduenas.es. Charge.
Named after the now-demolished neighbouring monastery Santa María de las Dueñas, this fifteenth- and sixteenth-century **palace** was originally home to the lords of Casa Beremeja. It was later inherited by the Marquis of Villanueva del Rio and in 1612, when his daughter married the future duke of Alba, Fernando Álvarez de Toledo, the house was passed to the Alba line.

Palacio de las Dueñas

Arco de la Macarena, outside La Basílica de la Macarena

It has belonged to the Casa de Alba ever since. In the nineteenth century, it served as a guesthouse and was the former home of the famous poet Antonio Machado who was born here in 1875. In the twentieth century, the exquisite Andalusian palace, with its ornate rooms and explosive bougainvillea, became a meeting point for international dignitaries and stars, from the likes of royalty to Jacqueline Kennedy.

Alameda de Hércules

MAP PAGE 66, POCKET MAP E3-4
Now a sprawling plaza laden with hip bars and restaurants, **Alameda de Hércules** looked very different just a few decades ago. Originally a small, stagnant lake within the city walls that was prone to flooding, the Conde de Barajas (essentially the mayor at the time) decided to drain the *laguna* and so built canals leading to the river. He then filled the space with statues, fountains and trees, effectively creating the first-ever urban garden in Europe. In the second half of the nineteenth century, the Alameda began to deteriorate along with the

neighbourhood – for a while it was nothing more than a stretch of dirt. However, in 2007, the city restored the plaza to what you see today. The square is dominated by a pair of Roman columns (only the south one is original), taken from Calle Mármoles in Santa Cruz, topped by statues of Hercules, said to be one of the founders of Seville, and Julius Caesar, who spent time in the city.

La Basílica de la Macarena

MAP PAGE 66, POCKET MAP F2
Pza. de la Esperanza Macarena 1. Free.
One of the most venerated Virgins in all of Seville – La Macarena – is tucked away in this 1949-built church. While the **basílica** is relatively new, the Catholic brotherhood presiding over the space was founded in 1595 by the *hortelanos* (farmers) de San Basílio. Just outside the church is the **Arco de la Macarena**, one of only three remaining city gates in the original walls, which served as the royal entryway for the kings and queens of the period. In front stands a statue of Joselito del Gallo, one of Seville's most famous bullfighters.

66

ALAMEDA, SAN LORENZO AND MACARENA

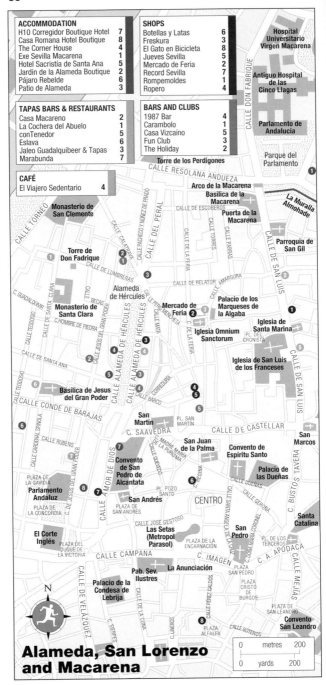

ACCOMMODATION
H10 Corregidor Boutique Hotel 7
Casa Romana Hotel Boutique 8
The Corner House 4
Exe Sevilla Macarena 1
Hotel Sacristía de Santa Ana 5
Jardin de la Alameda Boutique 2
Pájaro Rebelde 6
Patio de Alameda 3

SHOPS
Botellas y Latas 6
Freskura 3
El Gato en Bicicleta 8
Jueves Sevilla 5
Mercado de Feria 2
Record Sevilla 7
Rompemoldes 1
Ropero 4

TAPAS BARS & RESTAURANTS
Casa Macareno 2
La Cochera del Abuelo 1
conTenedor 5
Eslava 6
Jaleo Guadalquibeer & Tapas 3
Marabunda 7

BARS AND CLUBS
1987 Bar 4
Carambolo 1
Casa Vizcaíno 5
Fun Club 3
The Holiday 2

CAFÉ
El Viajero Sedentario 4

Alameda, San Lorenzo and Macarena

A wealthy gentlemen and devoted follower of La Macarena, Joselito himself bought the emblematic emeralds that hang on the Virgin's lace cloak while travelling through Paris. When he was killed in a bullfight, the brotherhood paraded the Virgin into the bullring dressed in mourning garb – the only time this has ever happened.

La Muralla Almohade

MAP PAGE 66, POCKET MAP F2
C/Macarena 22.
Next to the Arco de la Macarena lies the largest chunk of the ancient Moorish city walls – **La Muralla Almohade** – dating back to 1105. While you may spot smaller portions of the fortifications around town, this is by far the most impressive, punctuated with eight towers, narrow entryways and battlement-studded walkways. The city is currently restoring the structure and in time visitors will be able to climb the tower and walk along parts of the wall.

Basílica de Jesus del Gran Poder

MAP PAGE 66, POCKET MAP D4
Pza. San Lorenzo 13.
www.gran-poder.es. Free.
The Basílica de Jesus del Gran Poder in San Lorenzo houses Seville's most cherished statue of Jesus, in which Christ – dressed in an elaborate embroidered cloak – carries the cross in suffering. The intricate wooden image was carved in the seventeenth century by Juan de Mesa, one of the most recognized sculptors of this style of realistic religious art. During Holy Week, the statue is paraded through the streets.

Iglesia Omnium Sanctorum

MAP PAGE 66, POCKET MAP E3
C/Peris Mencheta 2.
www.omniumsanctorum.org. Charge.
While far less visited than most of Seville's churches, the **Iglesia Omnium Sanctorum** shelters the city's oldest standing church behind its rather unassuming facade. When the Christians conquered Seville in 1248, they built twenty-four churches in the city to mark their religious territory over the previous Muslim rule. The Iglesia Omnium Sanctorum was one of them.

Oddly enough, the architects held on to aspects of Moorish architecture, utilizing the Mudéjar design (notice the minaret tower and subtle tilework above the door) along with more imposing Gothic flourishes.

Mercado de Feria

MAP PAGE 66, POCKET MAP E3
C/Feria s/n.
Food market usually Mon–Sat 8am–midnight; flea market Thurs 9am–2pm.
Attached to the Iglesia Omnium Sanctorum, the eighteenth-century **Mercado de Feria** is the oldest food market in Seville. Opening hours are notoriously unreliable, though on any given day you will usually find at least a few tapas bars open and a smattering of food stalls piled high with fresh fruit, seasonal

Basílica de Jesus del Gran Poder

Iglesia de San Luis de los Franceses

veg, cured meats, local specialities and oven-fresh sweet treats. Every Thursday, colourful stalls spill along Calle Feria as the city's biggest flea market, or *mercadillo* (also known as **Jueves Market**), comes to life. The offering is eclectic: art, antiques, books, crockery, flamenco dresses, the odd vintage sewing machine or birdcage, and much more. It's a great place to stroll even if you don't buy anything; the vibe is lively, and you'll rub shoulders with locals browsing through the heaps of treasures.

Palacio de los Marqueses de la Algaba

MAP PAGE 66, POCKET MAP E3
Pza. Calderón de la Barca s/n.
955 472 525. Free.
Tucked behind the Mercado de Feria, the **Palacio de los Marqueses de la Algaba** is a fine example of Gothic Mudéjar architecture. Behind its grand facade, the fifteenth-century palace shelters the Mudéjar Art Interpretation Center, a small museum exhibiting over one hundred works from the twelfth to

the twentieth centuries. English-language information cards show how the art blends Christian and Islamic influences. A highlight is the display detailing how the intricate patterns on the adorning *azulejos* were created. The tranquil interior courtyard is often used to host cultural events.

Iglesia de San Luis de los Franceses

MAP PAGE 66, POCKET MAP F4
San Luis 37.
www.dipusevilla.es/sanluisdelosfranceses.
Charge, free for EU citizens.
Built between 1699 and 1731, the **Iglesia de San Luis de los Franceses** is an ancient Jesuit church sheltering one of the best-preserved Baroque enclaves in the city. Dedicated to King Louis IX of France, this circular temple is a dazzling display of gilt and carving. The eye-popping salmon-pink facade is etched with elaborate designs; the church's Solomonic columns along the altar are adorned with helical spirals and twists. The building was deconsecrated in 1835 and now hosts concerts and plays.

Shops

Botellas y Latas

MAP PAGE 66, POCKET MAP E5
C/Regina 15. 954 293 122.

Gourmand shop selling regional specialities like *jamón ibérico*, local cheeses, olive oil, jams and other suitcase-friendly goodies. Perfect for picking up an edible souvenir or gift.

Freskura

MAP PAGE 66, POCKET MAP E4
C/Vulcano 4. 954 373 089.

Ice cream is a necessity during the sweltering summer months, and the best can be found in an Italian-style gelato shop just off Alameda de Hércules. Seasonal fruit flavours like fig showcase local ingredients; summer grapefruit *granita* (shaved ice) takes the edge off the blistering midday sun; and near-perfect classic Italian specialities like pistachio, *nocciola* (hazelnut) and rich chocolate consistently hit the mark. Also has a selection of dairy-free options. Take a peek into the kitchen from the street to watch the team work their gelato magic.

El Gato en Bicicleta

MAP PAGE 66, POCKET MAP E6
C/Pérez Galdós 22. 955 295 651.

Inviting bookshop, café and art gallery hybrid, packed with the latest titles on interiors, design and poetry. Also has a pottery studio on site for classes.

Jueves Sevilla

MAP PAGE 66, POCKET MAP E4
C/Feria 40.

Right next door to neighbouring store *Ropero* (see page 70), *Jueves* is another excellent vintage store helping to cement Calle Feria as a thrifting hotspot. Secondhand gems include a pile of superb denim, leather jackets, oversized shirts and other wardrobe staples for the conscientious shopper.

Mercado de Feria

MAP PAGE 66, POCKET MAP E3
C/Feria s/n.

The city's biggest flea market (*mercadillo*) spills along Calle Feria every Thursday morning and showcases a treasure trove of antiques, along with curious secondhand trinkets and some particularly interesting characters.

Record Sevilla

MAP PAGE 66, POCKET MAP D5
C/Amor de Dios 17. 954 387 702.

Cool record store jam-packed with new and secondhand vinyl along with other retro goodies like CDs and cassettes, plus a selection of merch. A must-stop for avid music fans.

Rompemoldes

MAP PAGE 66, POCKET MAP F3
San Luís 70.

Artisanal hub where craftspeople breathe new life into age-old traditions, tinkering away in their workshops to create one-off gems like ceramics, jewellery, art and sculptures. Studios double up as shops where the makers exhibit and sell their works; many live above their workplaces in purpose-built apartments.

Mercado de Feria

Ropero

MAP PAGE 66, POCKET MAP E4

C/Feria 37.

Conscious fashionista María Alonso is the powerhouse behind *Ropero*, one of Seville's best thrift shops. This colourful store is packed to the rafters with vintage clothing, shoes and bags, and it's easy to lose a few hours browsing its rails.

Café

El Viajero Sedentario

MAP PAGE 66, POCKET MAP E4

Alameda de Hércules 77.

With mural-splashed walls and a tree-shaded courtyard, this lovely little literary café combines coffee and books to cosy effect. Serves home-baked treats like cakes and pastries plus breakfasts and light bites. Also hosts film screenings, live music and poetry readings.

Tapas bars and restaurants

Casa Macareno

MAP PAGE 66, POCKET MAP F3

Pza. Pumarejo 2. 955 417 299.

While a little rough around the edges, the Plaza Pumarejo is a hotspot for in-the-know locals thanks to its cluster of tapas bars and restaurants; you're unlikely to spot a fellow tourist here. *Casa Macareno* stands out among the competition for its simple formula: authentic tapas, excellent charcuterie and creative *montaditos* (small hand-held sandwiches). The croquettes are always a winner, along with the crispy squid *montadito* with aioli. €€

La Cochera del Abuelo

MAP PAGE 66, POCKET MAP D3

C/Álvaro de Bazán 2. 664 440 636.

An eighteenth-century carriage house has been reimagined as this intimate restaurant, sensitively restored with wooden shutters, soaring arches and antique furniture. The menu is loosely written and changes frequently, as dishes are built only on seasonal ingredients and the freshest catch. Don't miss the seafood-laden signature rice dish if it's on the agenda. €€€

conTenedor

MAP PAGE 66, POCKET MAP F4

San Luis 50. www.restaurantecontenedor.com.

Farm-to-fork restaurant abiding by the slow food ethos. The menu draws on the natural larder of Andalucía, prioritizing zero-kilometre ingredients and local organic and sustainable producers. Dishes are seasonal and might include snapper ceviche; wild grouper and vegetables with chamomile and salicornia; or papaya salad marinated in lentil caviar and ginger. €€€€

Eslava

MAP PAGE 66, POCKET MAP D4

C/Eslava 3. www.espacioeslava.com.

Behind the Basílica de Jesus del Gran Poder is one of the city's busiest and best tapas bars. Dishes range from ultra-traditional to out-of-the-box innovations, like the award-winning slow-cooked egg yolk perched on a wine-soaked boletus mushroom cake. A seat here is hard to come by, so be sure to make a reservation well in advance otherwise you risk missing out. €€

Jaleo Guadalquibeer & Tapas

MAP PAGE 66, POCKET MAP E3

Mercado Feria. 678 498 787.

From a simple seared cut of Ibérico pork to spicy, tuna-laden twists on *salmorejo* (the south's cold tomato soup), this humming stall in the Mercado de Feria is a great weekend lunch spot. The ever-changing menu leans towards market offerings, but keep a lookout for the Sunday paella. €

The legendary *Casa Vizcaíno*

Marabunda

MAP PAGE 66, POCKET MAP D5
Jesús del Gran Poder 31.
www.marabundafood.com.
In a light and airy setting, this lively neighbourhood joint slings Asian-inspired riffs on the classics, all brainstormed by chef Francis Balongo. Think slow-cooked pork cheeks stuffed into a brioche and slathered in kimchi mayo, or prawn croquettes with chili crab sauce. Don't miss the *bocata de solomillo al whisky* (pork tenderloin in a garlic-lashed whisky sauce). €€

Bars and clubs

1987 Bar

MAP PAGE 66, POCKET MAP E4
Alameda de Hércules 93.
This 80s-themed bar and dance club, with odes to Bowie and Queen painted on its garage doors, has a slightly more adult crowd than the youthful hordes that typically flock to the Alameda.

Carambolo

MAP PAGE 66, POCKET MAP E3
Alameda de Hércules 47. www.carambolo-sevilla-alameda.business.site.
It is reggaeton hits all night long at this small club at the end of the Alameda de Hércules. Hookah

lovers can also enjoy a smoke on the upstairs outdoor terrace.

Casa Vizcaíno

MAP PAGE 66, POCKET MAP E4
C/Feria 27. 954 38 60 57.
The legendary *El Vizcaíno* is the ideal place to start a bar crawl, with an icy local Cruzcampo beer or house vermouth in hand. From hippies to hipsters, *sevillanos* to suits, this storied drinking den on the sun-soaked Plaza Monte Síon may be the city's great equalizer.

Fun Club

MAP PAGE 66, POCKET MAP E4
Alameda de Hércules 86.
www.funclubsevilla.com.
Popular music and dance bar – favouring rock, reggae, hip-hop and salsa – with live bands. Check the website for the schedule.

The Holiday

MAP PAGE 66, POCKET MAP D4
Jesús de Gran Poder 73.
By far the neighbourhood's (and possibly Seville's) best club, *The Holiday* opened in 1975 – the same historic year the oppressive dictatorship ended in Spain. Reggaeton, modern pop and rock pumps out from DJ turntables, along with 80s and 90s tunes. Also hosts regular drag shows. Arrive late: this place is open until 7am.

Day-trips

While you could easily spend weeks exploring every hidden corner of Seville and hopping from one languid tapas bar terrace to the other, there's much to see outside the city. From small whitewashed villages to Gothic monasteries and archeological sites, as well a plethora of natural sights and hikes, day-trips open up a whole new understanding of how folks live (and lived) in this rich southern region of Spain. Take in the light-pricked coastlines of Cádiz, the Roman ruins at Itálica or the jaw-dropping arched bridge across the gorge in Ronda. Many towns can be reached by train or bus, but if you're looking to explore smaller villages (many of which are fairly close together) and hiking trails, a rental car is your best bet.

Itálica

MAP PAGE 76

Avda. de San Isidoro, Santiponce. www.italicasevilla.org. Charge, free with EU passport. Bus #M170A departs the Pza. de Armas station (every 30min, Sun every hour; 20min); it makes its way into Santiponce before turning back on itself and heading out of town again, where you get off at the Itálica stop. Buses return to Seville from this same stop.

The Roman amphitheatre at Itálica

The Roman ruins and remarkable mosaics of **Itálica** lie some 9km to the north of Seville, just outside the village of Santiponce, where also remain the well-preserved foundations of a Roman theatre. Itálica was the birthplace of two emperors (Trajan and Hadrian) and one of the earliest Roman settlements in Spain, founded in 206 BC by Scipio Africanus as a

Remarkable mosaics at Itálica

home for his veterans. It rose to considerable military importance in the second and third centuries AD, was richly endowed during the reign of Hadrian (117–138AD) and declined as an urban centre only under the Visigoths, who preferred Seville, then known as *Hispalis*. Eventually, the city was deserted by the Moors after the river changed its course, disrupting the surrounding terrain.

Throughout the Middle Ages, the ruins were used as a source of stone for Seville, but somehow the shell of its enormous amphitheatre – the third largest in the Roman world – has survived. Today, it's crumbling perilously, but you can clearly detect the rows of seats, the corridors and the dens for wild beasts. Beyond, within a rambling and unkempt grid of streets and villas, around twenty mosaics have been uncovered. Most are complete, including excellent coloured floors depicting birds, Neptune and the seasons, and several fine black-and-white geometric patterns. More recently, the site was used as a filming location for *Game of Thrones*.

Monasterio San Isidoro del Campo

MAP PAGE 76
Avda. de San Isidoro 18, Santiponce. 955 624 400. Free. Bus #M172 connects Pza. de Armas station in Seville (every 30min, Sun every hour; stop 41; 20min) and Santiponce.

A little over 1km to the south of Santiponce on the road back to Seville lies the former Cistercian **Monasterio San Isidoro del Campo**. Closed for many years, it was painstakingly and gloriously restored and shouldn't be missed. Founded in the fourteenth century by monarch Guzmán El Bueno of Tarifa, the monastery is a masterpiece of Gothic architecture, which, prior to its confiscation during the nineteenth-century Disentailment (government seizure of property), was occupied by a number of religious orders. Among these were the *ermitaños jerónimos* (Hieronymites) who, in the fifteenth century, decorated the central cloister and the Patio de los Evangelistas with a remarkable series of mural paintings depicting images of the saints – including scenes from the

Monasterio San Isidoro del Campo

life of San Jerónimo – as well as astonishingly beautiful floral and Mudéjar-influenced geometric designs. In the seventeenth century, the monastery employed the great *sevillano* sculptor Martínez Montañés to create the magnificent *retablo mayor* in the larger of the complex's twin churches.

Parque Nacional Coto de Doñana

MAP PAGE 76
Charge. 50min drive south of Seville; visits by 4WD tour only.

The province of Huelva stretches between Seville and Portugal. With a scenic section of the Sierra Morena to the north and a chain of fine beaches to the west of the provincial capital, it has a lot to offer but suffers a mixed reputation. This is probably because it's laced with large areas of swamp – the *marismas* – and is notorious for mosquitoes. This distinctive habitat is, however, particularly suited to a great variety of wildlife, especially birds, and over 60,000 acres of the delta of the Río Guadalquivir (the largest roadless area in western Europe) have been fenced off to

form the **Parque Nacional Coto de Doñana**. Here, amid sand dunes, pine woods, marshes and freshwater lagoons, live scores of flamingos, along with rare birds of prey, around 75 of the endangered Iberian lynx, mongooses and a startling variety of migratory birds.

The seasonal pattern of its delta waters, which flood in winter and then drop in the spring, leaving rich deposits of silt, raised sandbanks and islands, gives Coto de Doñana its uniqueness. Conditions are perfect in winter for ducks and geese, but spring is more exciting; the exposed mud draws hundreds of flocks of breeding birds. In the marshes and amid the cork-oak forests behind, you've a good chance of seeing squacco herons, black-winged stilts, whiskered terns, pratincoles and sand grouse, as well as flamingos, egrets and vultures. There are, too, occasional sightings of the Spanish imperial eagle, now reduced to a score of breeding pairs. Conditions are not so good in late summer and early autumn, when the *marismas* dry out and support far less birdlife.

It is no Iberian Arcadia, however, and given the region's parlous economic state the park is under constant threat from development. Even at current levels the drain on the water supply is severe, and made worse by pollution of the Guadalquivir by farming pesticides, Seville's industry and Huelva's mines. The seemingly inevitable disaster finally occurred in 1998 when an upriver mining dam used for storing toxic waste burst, unleashing millions of litres of pollutants into the Guadiamar, which flows through the park.

The noxious tide was stopped just two kilometres before the park's boundary, but surrounding farmland suffered catastrophic damage, with nesting birds decimated and fish poisoned. What is even more worrying is that

Exploring the white towns

From Ronda, almost any route to the north or west is rewarding, taking you past a whole series of white towns, many of them fortified since the days of the Reconquest from the Moors – hence the mass of "de la Frontera" suffixes. Perhaps the best of all the routes, though a roundabout one, and tricky without your own transport, is to Cádiz (see page 104) via Grazalema, Ubrique and Medina Sidonia. This passes through the spectacular Parque Natural de la Sierra de Grazalema before skirting the nature reserve of Cortes de la Frontera (which you can drive through by following the road beyond Benaoján) and, towards Alcalá de los Gazules, running through the northern fringe of Parque Natural de los Alcornocales, which derives its name from the forests of cork oaks, one of its main attractions and the largest of its kind in Europe.

the mining dams have not been removed (the mines are a major employer) but merely repaired.

In 2017, a large forest fire just 30km west of the park forced the evacuation of 2000 people. Though firefighters got the spread under control before it reached Doñana, one of the park's protected species, an Iberian lynx, died from stress. Some local people and environmental bodies are suspicious of arson by developers who they think have ulterior intentions for the area that's currently protected.

Nonetheless, Spain's largest nature reserve, its river delta, seasonal wetlands and ever-shifting dunes continues to provide a precious habitat for a huge diversity of birds and mammals, including many endangered species. A signpost indicates the national park visitor centre of El Acebuche. There is an exhibition about the flora and fauna of the reserve here and you

The flamingo-speckled lagoons of Parque Nacional Coto de Doñana

can follow two nature trails around nearby lagoons. To protect its fragile environment, access to the interior of the Doñana is restricted to organized tours, which can be booked either in person or, better still, in advance.

Ronda

MAP PAGE 76

A bus from Seville's Pza. de Armas bus station is the quickest way to get to Ronda, at about 2hr 15min.

The full natural drama of **Ronda**, rising amid a ring of dark, angular mountains, is best appreciated as you enter the town. Built on an isolated ridge of the sierra, it's split in half by a gaping river gorge, El Tajo, which drops sheer for 130m on three sides. Still more spectacular, the gorge is spanned by a stupendous eighteenth-century arched bridge, the Puente Nuevo, while tall, whitewashed houses lean from its precipitous edges.

Much of the attraction of Ronda lies in this extraordinary view, or in walking down by the Río Guadalvín, following one of the donkey tracks through the rich green valley. The town has a number of museums and, surprisingly, has sacrificed little of its character to the flow of day-trippers from the Costa del Sol. Ronda divides into three parts: on the south side of the bridge is the old Moorish town, La Ciudad, and farther south still, its San Francisco suburb. On the near north side of the gorge, and where you'll arrive by public transport, is the largely modern Mercadillo quarter.

La Ciudad retains intact its Moorish plan and a great many of its houses, interspersed with fine Renaissance mansions. It is so intricate a maze that you can do little else but wander at random. At the centre of La Ciudad, on Ronda's most picturesque square,

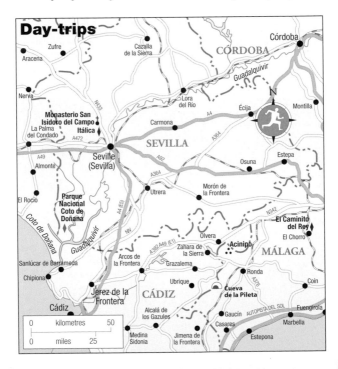

the Plaza Duquesa de Parcent, stands the cathedral church of Santa María La Mayor, originally the Moorish town's Friday mosque. Externally, it's a graceful combination of Moorish, Gothic and Renaissance styles with the belfry built on top of the old minaret. Climb this to reach the rooftop walkway for magnificent views of the town and countryside.

At some stage, make your way across the Puente Nuevo, peering down into the yawning Tajo and the Río Guadalvín, far below. The bridge was originally the town prison, and last saw use during the Civil War, when Ronda was the site of some of the south's most vicious massacres. Hemingway, in *For Whom the Bell Tolls*, recorded how prisoners were thrown alive into the gorge.

Near the southern end of La Ciudad are the ruins of the Alcázar, once impregnable until razed by the French in 1809. Beyond here, the principal gates of the town, the magnificent Moorish Puerta de Almocabar, through which passed the Christian conquerors (led personally by Fernando), and the triumphal Puerta de Carlos V, erected later during the reign of the Habsburg emperor, stand side by side at the entrance to the suburb of San Francisco.

The Mercadillo quarter, which grew up in the wake of the Reconquest, is of comparatively little interest, although it is now the town's commercial centre. There is only one genuine monument here, the eighteenth-century Plaza de Toros sited on Plaza Teniente Arce, close to the beautiful clifftop

Puente Nuevo in Ronda

walk, Paseo de Orson Welles, and offering spectacular views towards the Sierra de Ronda. Ronda played a leading part in the development of bullfighting and was the birthplace of the modern corrida (bullfight). The ring, built in 1781, is one of the earliest in Spain and the fight season here is one of the country's most important.

Acinipo

MAP PAGE 76
Free.

Some 12km northwest of Ronda are the ruins of a town and Roman theatre at a site locally known as **Ronda la Vieja**, reached by turning right 6km down the main A374 road to Arcos/Seville. At the site a friendly farmer, who is also the guardian, will present you with a plan (in Spanish). Based on

Ham it up

Aracena is at the heart of a prestigious *jamón*-producing area, so try to sample some of the dry-cured ham. Also look out for, when they're in season, the delicious wild asparagus and *setas* (wild mushrooms). Another prized delicacy are local snails, which are in the fields in summer.

Neolithic foundations – note the recently discovered prehistoric stone huts beside the entrance – it was as a Roman town in the first century AD that **Acinipo** (the town's Roman name) reached its zenith. Immediately west of the theatre, the site's most imposing ruin, the ground falls away in a startlingly steep escarpment offering fine views all around, taking in the picturesque hill village of Olvera to the north.

Cueva de la Pileta

MAP PAGE 76

Daily guided visits only. Charge; limit of 25 persons per tour, booking essential. www.cuevadelapileta.org. From Ronda, take either an Algeciras-bound local train to Estación Benaoján-Montejaque (3 daily; 20min), or a bus, which drops you a little closer in Benaoján.

West from Ronda is the prehistoric **Cueva de la Pileta**, a fabulous series of caverns with some remarkable paintings of animals (mainly bison), fish and what are apparently magic symbols. These etchings and the occupation of the cave date from about 25,000 BC – hence predating the more famous caves at Altamira in northern Spain – to the end of the Bronze Age. You can only visit the caves by guided tour, which lasts an hour on average, but can be longer, and is in Spanish – though the guide does speak a little English. There are hundreds of bats in the cave, and no artificial lighting, so visitors carry lanterns; you may also want to take a jumper, as the caves can be extremely chilly. Be aware if you leave a car in the car park that thieves are active here.

Olvera

MAP PAGE 76

From Ronda, Olvera is a 50min drive north on the A-374 and A-384.

Olvera is one of the largest of the white towns. Its silhouette is dramatic: a Moorish keep and the imposing Iglesia de la Encarnación rise above tightly packed houses sloping down to a clear perimeter where the countryside begins. Famous

Olvera, crowned by Iglesia de la Encarnación

as a refuge for outlaws in the nineteenth century, Olvera today has a reputation for excellent olive oil and religiosity. A monument to the Sacred Heart of Jesus on a natural outcrop of rock dominates the lower town, and pilgrims have been known to crawl for miles on their hands and knees, in fulfilment of a vow, to the popular sanctuary of the Virgen de los Remedios.

If you have time to spare you might like to walk or cycle along the Vía Verde de la Sierra (green way) that starts in Olvera. For 36km, it follows the route of a disused railway line to Puerto Serrano, passing through a vulture reserve on the way.

Grazalema

MAP PAGE 76
From Ronda, Grazalema is a 45min drive via the A-374 and A-372.

Just under 25km from Ronda is **Grazalema**, at the centre of the magnificent Parque Natural de la Sierra de Grazalema, a paradise for hikers and naturalists. A protected area of rugged terrain, the natural park has an unusual microclimate that's preserved some ancient Mediterranean forest and a precious wildlife habitat. The village itself is extremely pretty: a cascade of

Parque Natural de la Sierra de Grazalema

pretty whitewashed houses tucked into the folds of the foothills below San Cristóbal. It's a welcoming, ebullient place, despite laying claim to the region's highest rainfall.

Come winter, its wrought-iron balconies and geranium-filled window boxes are often coated with snow. Residents earn a living from ceramics and woollen products, crafted according to long-established traditions, as well as tourism. You can see traditional

The Roman ruins of Carmona

The extraordinary Roman necropolis lies on a low hill at the opposite end of Carmona; if you're walking out of town from San Pedro, take C/Enmedio, the middle street of three (parallel to the main Seville road) that leave the western end of Paseo del Estatuto and follow this for about 450m. Here, amid the cypress trees, more than nine hundred family tombs dating from the second century BC to the fourth century AD can be found. Enclosed in subterranean chambers hewn from the rock, the tombs are often frescoed and contain a series of niches in which many of the funeral urns remain intact. Some of the larger tombs have vestibules with stone benches for funeral banquets, and several retain carved family emblems (one is of an elephant, perhaps symbolic of long life). Most spectacular is the Tumba de Servilia – a huge colonnaded temple with vaulted side chambers. Opposite the site is a partly excavated amphitheatre.

80

weaving methods at the Museo
de Artesanía Textil (free; www.
mantasdegrazalema.com). The
Puerto de las Palomas (Pass of
the Doves – at 1350m the second
highest pass in Andalucía) rears up
behind the village.

Cross this (a superb half-day walk
or short drive), and you descend to
Zahara de la Sierra, an unassuming
little town that wraps itself like a
helter-skelter around an isolated,
sheer outcrop, twisting down from
the ruined twelfth-century castle at
its peak.

Ubrique

MAP PAGE 76
Ubrique is 40min from Grazalema by car.
From Grazalema, following the
scenic A2302 towards Ubrique
takes you through the southern
pocket of the Parque Natural de la
Sierra de Grazalema, a landscape
of dramatic vistas and lofty
peaks. The road snakes through
the charming ancient villages
of Villaluenga del Rosario and
Benaocaz, and offers plenty of
opportunities for hikes – perhaps
down Benaocaz's 6km-long paved
Roman road – along the way.

Arcos de la Frontera

Another of the region's white
towns, **Ubrique** is a natural
mountain fortress and was a
Republican stronghold in the
Civil War.

Today, it's a prosperous and
bustling town, owing its wealth
to the medieval guild craft of
leatherworking. The highly skilled
leatherworkers produce bags, purses
and accessories for many of the big
names (including Loewe, Louis
Vuitton and Gucci) at unmarked
workshops around the town.
These high-value products are then
whisked away to be sold in Madrid,
Paris, Rome and London. Shops
selling the output of numerous
other workshops (footwear and
bags, often at bargain prices) line
Avenida Dr Solís Pascual.

Arcos de la Frontera

MAP PAGE 76
**Arcos de la Frontera is around a 40min
drive northwest of Ubrique.**
Taken from the Moors in 1264
– an impressive feat, for it stands
high above the Río Guadalete on a
double crag and must have been a
wretchedly impregnable fortress –
sits **Arcos de la Frontera**, another
of the glorious white towns. This
dramatic location, enhanced by a
picturesque huddle of low, sugar-
cube houses and fine sandstone
churches, is considered one of the
most beautiful towns in Spain.

The streets of the town are,
if anything, more interesting,
with their mix of Moorish and
Renaissance buildings. At its heart
is the Plaza del Cabildo, easily
reached by following the signs for
the parador, which occupies one
side of it.

Flanking another two sides
are the castle walls and the large
Gothic-Mudéjar church of Santa
María de la Asunción; the last
side is left open, offering plunging
views to the river valley. Below
the town to the north lies Lago de
Arcos (actually a reservoir) where
locals go to cool off in summer.

Gruta de las Maravillas

Aracena

MAP PAGE 76

Morning bus routes from Seville to Aracena only run on the weekends. Otherwise, rent a car and take the E-803 north out of town and veer west on the N-433.

Some 90km northwest of Seville, **Aracena** is the highest town in the Sierra Morena – the longest of Spain's mountain ranges, extending almost the whole way across Andalucía. A substantial but pretty place, Aracena rambles partly up the side of a hill topped by the Iglesia del Castillo, a Gothic-Mudéjar church built by the Knights Templar around the remains of a Moorish castle. The town is flanked to the south and west by a small offshoot of the Sierra Morena – the Sierra de Aracena – a wonderfully verdant corner of Andalucía with wooded hills and villages with cobbled streets, which is perfect for hiking.

Aracena's principal attraction, along with its award-winning cured Spanish ham (*jamón ibérico*), is the Gruta de las Maravillas, the largest and arguably most impressive cave in Spain. Supposedly discovered by a local boy in search of a lost pig, the cave is now illuminated and there are guided tours as soon as a couple of dozen or so people have assembled. To protect the cave, there's a strict limit of forty persons per visit.

At weekends and holiday periods, try to visit before noon – coach parties with advance bookings tend to fill up the afternoon allocation. On Sunday, there's a constant procession, but usually plenty of time to gaze and wonder. The cave is astonishingly beautiful, and funny to visit, too – the last chamber of the tour is known as the Sala de los Culos (Room of the Buttocks), its walls and ceiling an outrageous, naturally sculpted exhibition, tinged in a pinkish-orange light.

Hikers can pick up useful information (including maps and leaflets) on the surrounding Parque Natural Sierra de Aracena y Picos de Aroche from an information centre in the ancient *cabildo* (town hall), Plaza Alta 5. You should also ask at the Aracena *turismo* for the free *Senderos de la Sierra de Aracena y Picos de Aroche* map, which lists 23 waymarked routes.

Carmona

Carmona

MAP PAGE 76

Buses from Seville leave from Avda. Kansas City and stop on the central Paseo del Estatuto in sight of the landmark ancient gateway, the Puerta de Sevilla.

Set on a low hill overlooking a fertile plain, **Carmona** is a small, picturesque town made recognizable by the fifteenth-century tower of the Iglesia de San Pedro, built in imitation of Seville's Giralda. The tower is the first thing you catch sight of upon arrival, and it sets the tone for the place – an appropriate one, since the town shares a similar history to Seville, less than 30km distant.

Carmona was an important Roman city (from which era it preserves a fascinating subterranean necropolis), and under the Moors was often governed by a brother of the Sevillan ruler. Later, Pedro the Cruel built a palace within its castle, which he used as a "provincial" royal residence.

To get your bearings, it's helpful to know that the town consists of the *casco antiguo* (old town) inside the walls entered through the impressive Puerta de Sevilla, and the more modern town to the west. The heart of the old quarter centres around the Plaza de San Fernando (often called the "Plaza Mayor") which, though modest in size, is dominated by a cluster of splendid Moorish-style buildings. Behind the square, and just to the south, there's a bustling local fruit and vegetable market held most mornings in the porticoed Plaza del Mercado.

The Iglesia de San Pedro is a good place to start exploring; its soaring tower, built in imitation of the Giralda and added a century later, dominates Carmona's main thoroughfare, Calle San Pedro. Inside, you will find a splendid Baroque sacristy by Figueroa.

From the Paseo del Estatuto, the modern town's main thoroughfare, looking east, you are rewarded with a fine view of the magnificent Moorish Puerta de Sevilla, a grand, fortified Roman double gateway (with substantial Carthaginian and Moorish elements) to the old town. The old town is circled by 4km of ancient walls, inside which a tangle of narrow streets wind ups past Mudéjar churches and Renaissance mansions.

Following Calle Martín López and its continuations east from Plaza de San Fernando for around five hundred metres will bring you to an imposing Roman gateway, the Puerta de Córdoba, where the town comes to an abrupt and romantic halt. This was the start of the ancient Córdoba road (once the mighty Via Augusta heading north to Zaragoza, Gaul and finally Rome itself, but now a dusty dirt track) which dropped down from here to cross the wide-open plain below. Following the road for a few kilometres will lead you to an impressive five-arched Roman bridge (see box, page 78), just visible on the plain.

Tapas bars and restaurants

Aracena

Restaurante Casas

Pozo La Nieve 37.
www.restaurantecasas.es.
One of Aracena's top three restaurants, *Casas* is sited near the Gruta de las Maravillas and is only open lunchtimes. All the pork-based dishes are excellent, as are the *jamón* and *salchichón* (salami); there are some interesting hot and cold soups that incorporate the latter. The best seats in the house are on the outdoor terrace. €€€€

Restaurante José Vicente

Avda. Andalucía 51.
www.restaurantecasas.es.
For a memorable splurge, this is the place to come. Here, at arguably Aracena's best restaurant, patrons gather to savour the five grades of *jabugo jamón ibérico* (black-pig ham) under the approving gaze of owner-chef José Vicente Sousa. The set menu, which often includes a mouthwatering *solomillo ibérico* (black-pig loin), is a good-value option. The *costillas de cerdo ibérico* (ribs) are excellent and the *helado de castañas* (chestnut ice cream) makes the perfect end to a feast. €€€€

Restaurante La Serrana

Pozo de la Nieve s/n. 959 127 613.
The third of the triumvirate of Aracena's top-notch restaurants, and located opposite *Casas*, this is another place where sierra cooking is at its best. All the pork dishes are recommended and there's a more affordable weekday set menu. €€€€

Arcos de la Frontera

Mesón Los Murales

Close to the church of San Pedro, Pza. de Boticas 1. 678 06 41 63.
One of the best low-priced restaurant options in Arcos's old

Restaurante Casas, one of Aracena's finest

town, with a pleasant outdoor dining terrace and traditional dishes of the sierra. €€

Taberna Jóvenes Flamencos

C/Dean Espinosa 11, near the Pza. del Cabildo. 657 133 552.

Lively and popular flamenco-themed bar with a terrace, offering well-prepared *raciones*. Dishes include *pulpo a la gallega* (octopus) and *secreto ibérico* (pork loin), and there are plenty of vegetarian options. Sometimes stages flamenco concerts. €€€

Ronda

Albacara

C/Tenorio 8.
www.hotelmontelirio.com/en/restaurant.

One of Ronda's smartest restaurants (dress up rather than down), with the finest food, is sheltered within the grand *Hotel Montelirio*. The emphasis lies on contemporary Mediterranean cuisine such as shrimp balls in cockle sauce or duck liver with pistachio jam and a reduction of Ronda wine. €€€€

Casa Ortega

Pza. del Socorro 17.
www.restauranteortega.es.

Popular restaurant run by a local family whose specials include *ensalada de tomate* (they grow their own variety – marvel at the size of them piled on the counter) and home-reared roast kid goat. €€€

Entrevinos

C/del Pozo 2. 672 284 146.

Tiny venue with bar stools only, so pull up a pew and join the locals at the best place in town for locally produced Ronda wines paired with delicious tapas. You'll be spoiled for choice here: the wine list runs to nearly one hundred varieties, and there's an excellent selection of small plates, including the highly recommended *fideos negros* (black noodles). Local craft beers also available for those who aren't partial to wine. €€

Grazalema is littered with terrace restaurants

Parador de Ronda

Pza. de España. www.paradores.es.

The parador's upmarket restaurant unsurprisingly has an excellent choice of local and regional dishes such as *rabo de toro* (bull's tail) and *solomillo de ciervo* (venison loin). Dinner is, of course, served with a side of fine views. €€€€

Restaurante Almocábar

Ruedo de Alameda 5. 952 875 977.

Fine-dining restaurant with a pleasant outdoor dining terrace for sun-kissed afternoons. The menu is packed with creative variations on regional dishes, along with a range of fresh, seasonal salads such as the *ensalada almocábar*, which includes figs, cheese, pears and honey. House specials include *paté de perdiz* (partridge) and *cochinillo* (suckling pig). Reservations advised to avoid disappointment; it's a popular spot. €€€€

Siempre Igual

C/San José 2. 687 153 867.

This unassuming little drinking den, conveniently just a stone's throw from the bus station, complements its simple and delicious food with a great selection of regional wines. A local favourite, and a good spot to pass the time while waiting for a bus. €€

Grazalema

Cádiz El Chico

Pza. de España 8. 956 132 067.

Located on Grazalema's main square, *Cádiz El Chico* is one of the town's better restaurants. The kitchen specializes in the traditional cuisine of the sierra, so you can expect lots of roasted meats such as *cordero al horno de leña* (lamb roasted in a wood-fired oven), a signature dish of the restaurant. It also does a good line in tasty tapas and ice-cold beer in its bar. €€€

Parador de Ronda

El Torreón

C/Agua 44. 956 132 313.

El Torreón is a reliable and centrally located traditional restaurant specializing in hearty, meat-heavy dishes of the sierra, including game and venison when in season and *sopa de grazalema* (a filling mountain soup). There is usually also a handful of fish dishes and salads. The wine list is fairly priced, and you can eat in the inviting dining room upstairs or, in better weather, on a streetside terrace below. €€€

Ubrique

El Laurel de Miguel

C/San Juan Bautista 7,
just behind the main street.
www.ellaureldemiguel.com.

Good tapas and *raciones* bar with a decent range of wines plus a pleasant little street terrace for sun-soaked days. Try the *pluma ibérica* (pork loin) or *magret de pato* (duck breast). €€€

Córdoba

Córdoba lies upstream from Seville beside a loop of the Guadalquivir, which was once navigable as far as here. Historically, it was the largest city of Roman Spain, and for three centuries it formed the heart of the western Islamic empire, the great medieval caliphate of the Moors. It is from this era that the city's major monument dates: the Mezquita, the grandest and most beautiful mosque ever constructed by the Moors in Spain. Famed for its tremendous and often wildly extravagant courtyards, Córdoba pushes this architectural form with a Festival of the Patios in May. Between the Mezquita and Avenida del Gran Capitán lies La Judería, Córdoba's old Jewish quarter, and a fascinating tangle of winding lanes – more atmospheric and less commercialized than Seville's Santa Cruz *barrio*, though tacky souvenir shops are beginning to gain ground. Just 7km outside the town, more Moorish splendours are to be seen among the ruins of the extravagant palace complex of Medina Azahara.

Córdoba, home to the magnificent Mezquita

Getting to Córdoba

Reaching Córdoba from Seville by public transport is a cinch. The fastest way is by high-speed AVE train (28 daily), which departs from Santa Justa station and takes just 45min (1hr 20min by regional train). You'll arrive at Córdoba's splendid combined train and bus station on Plaza de las Tres Culturas, Avda. de América, at the northern end of town. From here, a 15min walk east towards Avda. del Gran Capitán will lead down to the old quarters and the Mezquita, or hop on bus #3 from outside the station. The cheapest option, however, is to travel by bus (3 daily; 2hr), departing from Seville's Plaza de Armas Station. Driving takes 1hr 40min and is an easy route along the A4, but arriving by car can be a pain, especially during rush hour in the narrow streets around the Mezquita. Parking in the centre is also a major headache, and it's worth considering staying somewhere that doesn't require traversing the old quarter. Better still is if you park up for the duration of your stay – Avda. de la República Argentina bordering the Jardines de la Victoria on the western edge of the old quarter, and across the river in the streets either side of the *Hotel Hespería Córdoba* are possible places – and then get around the city on foot, which is both easy and enjoyable.

Mezquita

MAP PAGE 88
Charge; free entrance for services at side doors Mon–Sat 8.30–9.30am, but without lighting. 957 470 512.

The development of the **Mezquita** paralleled the new heights of confidence and splendour of ninth- and tenth-century Córdoba. Abd ar-Rahman III provided it with a new minaret (which has not survived but provided the core for the later belfry), 80m high, topped by three pomegranate-shaped spheres, two of silver and one of gold and each weighing a tonne. But it was his son, al-Hakam II (r.961–76), to whom he passed on a peaceful and stable empire, who was responsible for the most brilliant expansion. He virtually doubled its extent, demolishing the south wall to add fourteen extra rows of columns, and employed Byzantine craftsmen to construct a new *mihrab*, or prayer niche; this remains complete and is perhaps the most beautiful example of all Moorish religious architecture.

Al-Hakam had extended the mosque as far to the south as was possible. The final enlargement of the building, under the chamberlain-usurper al-Mansur (r.977–1002), involved adding seven rows of columns to the whole east side. This spoiled the symmetry of the mosque, depriving the *mihrab* of its central position, but Arab historians observed that it meant there were now "as many bays as there are days of the year". They also delighted in describing the rich interior, with its 1293 marble columns, 280 chandeliers and 1445 lamps. Hanging inverted among the lamps were the bells of the pilgrimage Catedral de Santiago de Compostela. Al-Mansur made his Christian captives carry them on their shoulders from Galicia – a process that was to be observed in reverse after Córdoba was captured by Fernando el Santo (the Saint) in 1236.

As in Moorish times, the Mezquita is approached through the **Patio de los Naranjos**, a classic Islamic ablutions court

Patio de los Naranjos

that preserves its orange trees, although the fountains for ritual purification before prayer are now purely decorative. Originally, when in use for the Friday prayers, all nineteen naves of the mosque were open to this court, allowing the rows of interior columns to appear an extension of the trees with brilliant shafts of sunlight filtering through. Today, all but one of the entrance gates is locked and sealed, and the mood of the building has been distorted from the open and vigorous simplicity of the mosque to the mysterious half-light of a cathedral. Nonetheless, a first glimpse inside the Mezquita is immensely exciting. The mass of supporting pillars was, in fact, an early and sophisticated innovation to gain height. The original architect had at his disposal columns from the old Visigothic cathedral and from numerous Roman buildings; they could

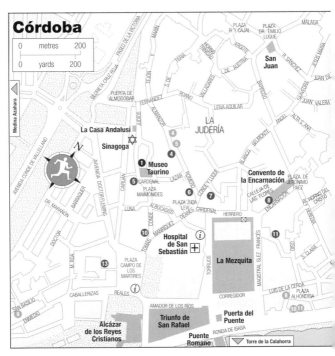

bear great weight but were not tall enough to reach the intended ceiling height. His solution (possibly inspired by Roman aqueduct designs) was to place a second row of square columns on the apex of the lower ones, serving as a base for the semicircular arches that support the roof. For extra strength and stability (and perhaps also deliberately to echo the shape of a date palm, much revered by the early Spanish Arabs), the architect introduced another, horseshoe-shaped arch above the lower pillars. A second and purely aesthetic innovation was to alternate brick and stone in the arches, creating the red-and-white-striped pattern that gives a unity and distinctive character to the whole design.

The uniformity was broken only at the culminating point of the mosque – the domed cluster of pillars surrounding the sacred

The glorious arches of the Mezquita

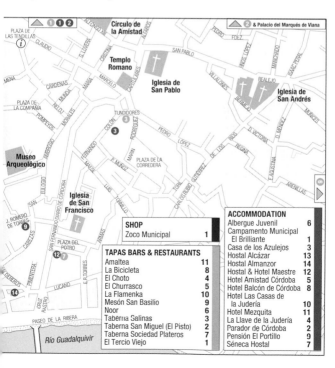

SHOP

Zoco Municipal	1

TAPAS BARS & RESTAURANTS

Amaltea	11
La Bicicleta	8
El Choto	4
El Churrasco	5
La Flamenka	10
Mesón San Basilio	9
Noor	6
Taberna Salinas	3
Taberna San Miguel (El Pisto)	2
Taberna Sociedad Plateros	7
El Tercio Viejo	1

ACCOMMODATION

Albergue Juvenil	6
Campamento Municipal El Brilliante	1
Casa de los Azulejos	3
Hostal Alcázar	13
Hostal Almanzor	14
Hostal & Hotel Maestre	12
Hotel Amistad Córdoba	5
Hotel Balcón de Córdoba	8
Hotel Las Casas de la Judería	10
Hotel Mezquita	11
La Llave de la Judería	4
Parador de Córdoba	2
Pensión El Portillo	9
Séneca Hostal	7

mihrab, erected under al-Hakam II. The **mihrab** has two functions in Islamic worship: it indicates the direction of Mecca (and hence of prayer) and it amplifies the words of the imam, or prayer leader. At Córdoba, it is also of supreme beauty. The inner vestibule of the niche (frustratingly fenced off) is quite simple in comparison, with a shell-shaped ceiling carved from a single block of marble. The chambers to either side – decorated with exquisite Byzantine mosaics of gold, rust red, turquoise and green – constitute the *maksura*, where the caliph and his retinue would pray.

Originally, the whole design of the mosque would have directed worshippers naturally towards the *mihrab*. Today, though, you almost stumble upon it, for in the centre of the mosque squats a Renaissance **Catedral coro**. This was built in 1523 – nearly three centuries of enlightened restraint after the Reconquest – and despite fierce opposition from the town council. The erection of a *coro* and *capilla mayor*, however, had long been the "Christianizing" dream of the Catedral chapter and at last they had found a monarch – predictably, Carlos V – who was willing to sanction the work. Carlos, to his credit, realized the mistake (though it did not stop him from destroying parts of the Alhambra and Seville's Alcázar); on seeing the work completed, he told the chapter, "You have built what you or others might have built anywhere, but you have destroyed something that was unique in the world." To the left of the *coro* stands an earlier and happier Christian addition – the Mudéjar **Capilla de Villaviciosa**, built by Moorish craftsmen in 1371 (and now partly sealed up). Beside it are the dome and pillars of the earlier *mihrab*, constructed under Abd ar-Rahman II.

The **belfry**, the **Torre del Alminar** at the corner of the Patio de los Naranjos, is contemporary with the Catedral addition and well worth a climb for the view of the patio and the Guadalquivir. Close by, the **Puerta del Perdón**, the main entrance to the patio, was rebuilt in Moorish style in 1377. It's worth making a tour of the Mezquita's **outer walls** before leaving; parts of the original caliphal decoration surrounding the portals (in particular, some exquisite lattice work) are stunning.

Torre de la Calahorra

MAP PAGE 88
Puente Romano s/n. Charge. 957 293 929.

At the eastern end of the Roman bridge over the Guadalquivir, the medieval **Torre de la Calahorra**

Pretty patios

Córdoba's old quarter, a compact warren of whitewashed houses, winding alleys and flower-filled patios, is best explored on foot. The houses generally present a blank facade to the street, broken only by an entryway closed by a *cancela*, a wrought-iron gate. Through this gate is glimpsed a patio, often shaded by a palm, furnished with ferns, perfumed with jasmine and air-conditioned by a fountain. Whether the intimate heart of private homes or elegant courtyards of great buildings, the patio was developed as a survival technique – a cool oasis in the long, hot summers. Fine examples can be seen in Calle San Basilio and around Plaza de la Magdalena in the district of Santa Marina. Córdoba celebrates its courtyards in May, when many private patios are opened to the public, an event on UNESCO's Intangible Cultural Heritage list.

Plaza de la Corredera

houses a gimmicky, high-tech museum containing models of the pre-cathedral Mezquita, peculiar talking tableaux and a rather incongruous multimedia presentation on the history of man. There's a great panoramic view, though, from the top of the tower towards the city. As you cross the bridge you can see, near the western riverbank, the wheels and the ruined mills that were in use for several centuries after the fall of the Muslim city, grinding flour and pumping water up to the fountains of the Alcázar.

Alcázar de los Reyes Cristianos

MAP PAGE 88
Pza. Campo Santo de los Mártires s/n.
Charge, free Thurs from 6pm (from noon June 16–Sept 15). 957 420 151.
After the Christian conquest, Córdoba's Alcázar was rebuilt a little to the west by Fernando and Isabel, hence its name, **Alcázar de los Reyes Cristianos**. The buildings are a bit dreary, having served as the residence of the Inquisition from 1428 to 1821, and later as a prison until 1951. However, they display some fine mosaics and other relics from Roman Córdoba, among which is one of the largest complete Roman mosaics in existence, and the wonderful **gardens** are a pleasant place to sit.

Plaza de la Corredera

MAP PAGE 88
To the northeast of the Mezquita, in an area that was once the *plateros* or silversmiths' quarter, you'll find **Plaza de la Corredera**, a wonderfully refurbished colonnaded square, much resembling Madrid's or Salamanca's Plaza Mayor. Unique in Andalucía, the square's complete enclosure occurred in the seventeenth century and presented the city with a suitable space for all kinds of spectacles. These included burnings by the Inquisition as well as bullfights, from which spectacle the tiny **Callejón Toril** (Bull Pen) on the square's eastern side takes its name. Now, bars and restaurants line the plaza, and their terraces are popular places to sit out on summer evenings.

Puerta de Almodóvar, an ancient city gate

La Judería

MAP PAGE 88

The area northwest of the Mosque is Córdoba's medieval Jewish quarter, **La Judería**, entered through the Puerta de Almodóvar, one of the city's ancient gates. If Córdoba is known for the splendour of its tenth-century achievements in art, architecture and science, a part of its glory is attributed to the Sephardim community, the Spanish Jews who settled here during the time of the Roman emperors, when they were allowed the same rights as other inhabitants of Baetica, Roman Spain. Under the Visigoths, Jews were persecuted so severely that they welcomed the Muslim invaders. In exchange, they enjoyed long periods of peaceful coexistence, and a flourishing Sephardic culture during which many achieved rare heights in diplomacy, medicine, commerce and crafts.

Near the Sinagoga (see below), the **Casa de Sefarad** (Calle Judíos; www.lacasadesefarad.com) is a fascinating museum focusing on the life of Spanish Jews. A little further, the **Casa Andalusí** (Calle Judíos 12; www.lacasaandalusi.es), a very pretty twelfth-century house with Islamic decoration and an exhibition on paper-making.

Sinagoga

MAP PAGE 88
C/Judíos 20. Charge, free with EU passport. 957 749 015.

Near the heart of La Judería is a **sinagoga**, one of only three synagogues in Spain – the other two are in Toledo – that survived the Jewish expulsion of 1492. This one, built in 1316, is minute, particularly in comparison with the great Santa María in Toledo, but it has some fine stuccowork elaborating on a Solomon's seal motif and retains its women's gallery. Outside is a statue of Maimónides, the Jewish philosopher, physician and Talmudic jurist, born in Córdoba in 1135.

Museo Taurino

MAP PAGE 88
Pza. de Maimónides s/n.
Charge, free Thurs from 6pm.

The small **Museo Taurino** (Bullfighting Museum) warrants a look, if only for the kitschy nature of its exhibits: row upon row of bulls' heads, two of them given this "honour" for having killed matadors. Beside a copy of the tomb of Manolete – most famous of the city's *toreros* – is exhibited the hide of his taurine nemesis, Islero. Adjacent to the museum is the richly decorated Chapel of San Bartolomé.

Museo Arqueológico

MAP PAGE 88
Pza. de Jerónimo Páez. Charge, free with EU passport. 957 355 517.

The **Museo Arqueológico** is in two buildings, one new and the other its first refurbished home, the beautiful sixteenth-century mansion of Casa Páez, which has a basement viewing area that

Visiting Medina Azahara

Visitors to the Medina Azahara (see page 94) must arrive at the Centro de Interpretación and take the dedicated bus (every 10–20min; charge) for the 2km journey to the site; once you have your ticket you can walk to the site, but it is all uphill. To reach Medina Azahara from Córdoba, city buses #01 and #02 from a stop on the Avda. de la República Argentina (at the northern end, near a petrol station) will drop you off at the intersection (cross the road with extreme care) from where it's a 1km walk. Ask the driver for "El Cruce de Medina Azahara". A special bus service also links Córdoba with the site. The bus departs from a signed stop on the Glorieta (roundabout) Cruz Roja at the southern end of Paseo de la Victoria (confirm this at the tourist office), but tickets must be purchased in advance from any municipal tourist office kiosk. Alternatively, a taxi will cost you about €30 one-way for up to five people, or there's a round-trip deal ("Taxi-Tour Córdoba"), which includes a 1hr wait at the site while you visit. A convenient taxi rank is located outside the *turismo* on the west side of the Mezquita. If you're driving, you are obliged to park your car at the Centro de Interpretación and take the bus to the site.

incorporates the *grados* (seats) of the Roman theatre both it and the mansion are built on top of. The museum exhibits an extensive Moorish collection, and well-presented Iberian and Roman sculptures as well as caliphal ceramics and *azulejos*.

Plaza del Potro starred in *Don Quixote*

Plaza del Potro

MAP PAGE 88

Near the river is **Plaza del Potro**, a fine old square named after the colt (*potro*) that adorns its restored fountain. This, as a wall plaque proudly points out, is mentioned in *Don Quixote*, and indeed Cervantes

Palacio del Marqués de Viana

himself is reputed to have stayed at the inn opposite, the **Posada del Potro**, which has an atmospheric cattle yard within.

The restored building is currently used as a centre for the study of flamenco and stages exhibitions and sporadic concerts.

Palacio del Marqués de Viana

MAP PAGE 88
Pza. de Don Gome 2. Charge. 957 496 741.
In the north of town are numerous Renaissance churches – some converted from mosques, others showing obvious influence in their minarets – and a handful of convents and palaces. The best of these, still privately owned although not by the family, is the **Palacio del Marqués de Viana**, whose main attraction for many visitors is its twelve flower-filled patios. The house itself – an ongoing work started in the fourteenth century – is mildly interesting and the guided tour (in Spanish only) leads you through drawing rooms, gaudy bedrooms (one with a telling Franco portrait), kitchens and galleries while pointing out furniture, paintings, weapons and top-drawer junk the family amassed over the centuries.

Medina Azahara

MAP PAGE 88
Charge, free with EU passport but a ticket still needs to be collected. 958 918 029.
Seven kilometres to the northwest of Córdoba lie the vast and rambling ruins of **Medina Azahara**, a palace complex built on a dream scale by Caliph Abd al-Rahman III. Naming it after a favourite, az-Zahra (the Radiant), he spent one-third of the annual state budget on its construction each year from 936 until his death in 961. Ten thousand workers and 1500 mules and camels were employed on the project, and the site, almost 2km long by 900m wide, stretched over three descending terraces. In addition to the palace buildings, it had a zoo, an aviary, four fish ponds, three hundred baths, four hundred houses, weapons factories and two barracks for the royal guard. Visitors, so the chronicles record, were stunned by its wealth and brilliance: one conference room

was decorated with pure crystals, creating a rainbow when lit by the sun; another was built round a huge pool of mercury.

For centuries following its downfall the Medina Azahara continued to be looted for building materials; parts, for instance, were used in Seville's Alcázar. But in 1944 excavations unearthed the remains of a crucial part of the palace – the **Royal House**, where guests were received and meetings of ministers held. This has been meticulously reconstructed and, though still fragmentary, its main hall must rank among the greatest of all Moorish rooms. It has a different kind of stuccowork from that at Granada or Seville – closer to natural and animal forms in its intricate Syrian Hom (Tree of Life) motifs. Unlike the later Spanish Arab dynasties, the Amazigh Almoravids and the Almohads of Seville, the caliphal Andalusians were little worried by Islamic strictures on the portrayal of nature, animals or even people – the beautiful hind in the Córdoba museum is a good example – and it may well have been this aspect of the palace that led to such zealous destruction during the Civil War.

The reconstruction of the palace gives a scale and focus to the site. Elsewhere, you have little more than foundations to stoke the imagination, amid an awesome area of ruins, hidden beneath bougainvillea and rustling with cicadas. Perhaps the most obvious of the outbuildings yet excavated is the **Aljama mosque**, just beyond the Royal House, which sits at an angle to the rest of the buildings in order to face Mecca.

After an extensive study of soil samples by biologists from Córdoba University to ascertain which plants and flowers would have originally been cultivated in the extensive **gardens**, reconstructive planting took place and the trees, shrubs and herbs are now maturing into a delightful and aromatic garden the caliphs would recognize.

The ruins of palace complex Medina Azahara

Shop

Zoco Municipal

MAP PAGE 88

C/Judíos s/n. 957 290 575.

At the top of Calle Judíos is the Zoco Municipal, a cluster of craft workshops huddled around a central courtyard. Its artisans work in both traditional and modern styles, in silver filigree (for which Córdoba has long been famous), leather, wood and ceramics.

Tapas bars and restaurants

Amaltea

MAP PAGE 88

C/Ronda de Isasa 10. www.amaltea.es.

Excellent organic restaurant with special veggie and coliac menus, run by a charming Wolverhampton-educated *cordobesa*. Specialities of the house include *couscous con verduras* (vegetables). Plenty of organic wines and a few special beers, too – try the Alhambra 1925. €€€

La Bicicleta

MAP PAGE 88

C/Cardenal González 1. 666 544 690.

Dinky café-bar with bike-themed decor, serving salads, snacks, cheese boards, juices and yoghurts plus some delicious home-made cakes. €

El Choto

MAP PAGE 88

C/Almanzor 10.

www.restauranteelchotocordoba.es.

Attractive, small and serious restaurant with a little outdoor terrace offering a range of well-prepared rice (twelve types), fish and meat dishes, including its delicious signature dish *choto asado* (roast kid). €€€

El Churrasco

MAP PAGE 88

C/Romero 16 (not C/Romero Barros).

www.elchurrasco.com.

This renowned restaurant, with a string of attractive dining rooms and outdoor patio, is famous for its fine *churrasco* (a grilled pork dish, served with punchy pepper sauce) and Córdoban local dish *salmorejo* (chilled tomato soup). €€€€

Zoco Municipal, a cluster of workshops around a courtyard

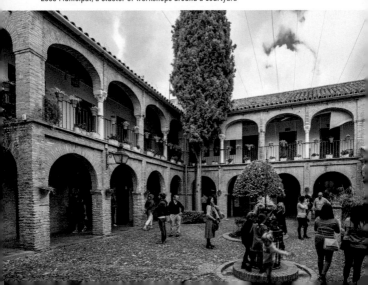

La Flamenka

MAP PAGE 88

Ronda de Isasa 10. 957 472 275.

On the fashionable riverfront and popular with a younger crowd, this restaurant combines traditional local cuisine with innovative modern twists, so you can dine on *salmorejo* and *berenjenas con miel* (aubergines with honey) with *bacalao carbón* (coal cod – don't be put off by the name). €€€€

Mesón San Basilio

MAP PAGE 88

C/San Basilio 19. 957 297 007.

Good, unpretentious and busy local restaurant offering decent fish and meat *raciones* and *platos combinados*, plus weekday menus. €€

Noor

MAP PAGE 88

C/Pablo Ruiz Picasso 8.

www.noorrestaurant.es.

Córdoba's hottest chef, Paco Morales, demonstrates his unique take on Andalusian cuisine in this two-Michelin-starred restaurant. There's a good-value set menu, but the two tasting menus take you on a journey to the city's gastronomic past where traditional ingredients such as aubergines, snails, lamb and almonds undergo a very modern transformation. €€€€

Taberna Salinas

MAP PAGE 88

C/Tundidores 3. www.tabernasalinas.com.

Reasonably priced taberna established in 1879, with dining rooms around a charming patio. Good *raciones* – try the *naranjas con bacalao* (cod with oranges) – and it serves a great *salmorejo*. €€€

Taberna San Miguel (El Pisto)

MAP PAGE 88

Pza. San Miguel 1. 957 470 166.

Known to all as *El Pisto* (the ratatouille), this is one of the city's legendary bars – over a century

Noor, worthy of two Michelin stars

old. Wonderful tapas: *rabo de toro* (oxtail stew), *potaje de garbanzos con manitas* (chickpea stew with trotters) and ratatouille are house specials. €€

Taberna Sociedad Plateros

MAP PAGE 88

C/San Francisco 6.

www.tabernaplateros.com.

This tapas bar, over a century old, serves a wide range of tapas – house specials include *arroz con bacalao* (cod paella) and *perdiz en escabeche* (marinated partridge). The bar is light and airy with a glass-covered patio complemented by hanging plants and *azulejos*. €€

El Tercio Viejo

MAP PAGE 88

C/Enrique Redel 17. 675 937 379.

Handy for the Palacio de Viana, this local bar serves traditional tapas and *raciones* such as *rabo de toro* and *callos con chorizo* (tripe with chorizo) and the Córdoban delicacy, *caracoles* (snails, served in spicy broth in a large cup). €€

Jerez de la Frontera

South of Seville is the home and heartland of sherry (itself an English corruption of the town's Moorish name – *Xerez*) and also of Spanish brandy. An elegant town with a lovely central area, Jerez de la Frontera is a tempting place to linger, arrayed as it is round the scores of *bodegas* and restaurants. You can't visit Jerez without signing up for a tour and tasting to sample the bounty of the land, though for an insight into local life, duck inside the city's *tabancos*. Elsewhere, a museum celebrates wine and specialty stores are lined with bottles. There are plenty of sights to visit in between the vititourism, from the Alcázar just south of the Plaza del Arenal to the Royal Andalusian School of Equestrian Art where you can see native horses – a great source of pride – perform to music. Life is lived at a sedate pace for most of the year here, though things liven up considerably when Jerez launches into one or other of its two big festivals – the May Horse Fair, or the celebration of the vintage towards the end of September.

Catedral de San Salvador

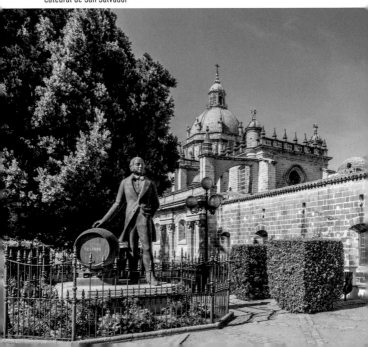

Getting to Jerez de la Frontera

From Seville, it is 1hr 15min by train (13 daily) to Jerez de la Frontera. The train station, *estación de ferrocarril*, is at Plaza de la Estación s/n, a 10min walk east of the town's central square, Plaza del Arenal, or a short bus ride (#10) from outside the station. Taking the bus from Seville is only marginally longer (12 daily; 1hr 30min) but cheaper. Jerez's bus station, *estación de autobuses*, is next to the train station. If you arrive by car, you'll meet the familiar problem of finding a place to park; to avoid being clamped or towed, use the pay car parks signed in the centre or park farther out and walk in. There is a huge underground car park beneath the central Plaza del Arenal. Jerez also has an airport (7km out of town on the NIV), with three daily buses to the centre and its own train station (on the opposite side of the airport car park) offering connections to Jerez central station. A taxi from the airport costs approximately €25–30 depending on traffic and the time of day.

Centro Andaluz de Flamenco

MAP PAGE 100
Pza. de San Juan. Free.
www.centroandaluzdeflamenco.es.

Jerez is famous throughout Spain for a long and distinguished flamenco tradition, and if you're interested in finding out more about Andalucía's great folk art, then a visit to the **Centro Andaluz de Flamenco** in the atmospheric *gitano* quarter, the Barrio de Santiago, is a must. There's an audiovisual introduction to *El Arte Flamenco* (hourly on the half-hour), plus videos of past greats and information on flamenco venues in the town.

The Alcázar

MAP PAGE 100
Charge.

The substantial **Alcázar** lies just to the south of the town's main square. To reach the entrance, take a right off the southern end of Plaza del Arenal into Plaza Monti, at the end of which you turn left into Calle María González. The entrance lies uphill on the left. Constructed in the twelfth century by the Almohads, though much altered since, the Alcázar has been extensively excavated and restored in recent years. The **gardens** have received particular attention: the plants and arrangements have been modelled as closely as possible – using historical research – on the original. The interior contains a

The Alcázar gardens

The elegant facade of the Catedral

well-preserved mosque complete with *mihrab*, now sensitively restored to its former state after having been used as a church for many centuries. The eighteenth-century **Palacio de Villavicencio** constructed on the west side of the Alcázar's Patio de las Armas (parade ground) houses an entertaining **camera obscura** offering views of the major landmarks of the town as well as the sherry vineyards and the sea beyond.

Catedral de San Salvador

MAP PAGE 100
Charge.

The eighteenth-century **Catedral de San Salvador** was rather harshly dismissed by Victorian British hispanist Richard Ford as "vile Churrigueresque" because of its mixture of Gothic and Renaissance styles, but an elegant facade – largely the work of

Jerez de la Frontera

BODEGAS
Bodegas Sandeman	1
Bodegas Tradición	2
González Byass	3

ACCOMMODATION
Albergue Juvenil	6
Hotel Al Andalus	4
Hotel Bellas Artes	1
Hotel Doña Blanca	3
Hotel-Hostal San Andrés	2
Pensión Las Palomas	5

TAPAS BARS & RESTAURANTS
El Almacén	4
Bar Juanito	5
La Carboná	3
La Condesa	1
Tabanco Plateros	2

Museo Arqueológico

Spanish Baroque architect Vicente Acero – is not without merit. Inside, over-obvious pointing gives the building an unfinished, breeze-block aspect, while, in the sacristy museum, there's a fine, little-known painting by Zurbarán – *The Sleeping Girl*. The most exciting time to be here is September, when on the broad steps of the Catedral, below the freestanding bell tower – actually part of an earlier, fifteenth-century Mudéjar castle – the wine harvest celebrations begin with the crushing of grapes.

Museo Arqueológico

MAP PAGE 100

Pza. del Mercado. Charge including useful English-language audio-guide (exhibit information is in Spanish only); free first Sun of each month.

The city's excellent **Museo Arqueológico** (Archeological Museum) lies five minutes north of the town centre on the edge of the Barrio de Santiago.

Bounty of the vines

An aristocrat among wines, sherry is produced from grapes grown in the chalky vineyards around Jerez de la Frontera. It is aged in casks by blending the young wine with a transfusion of mature sherry, a method known as *solera*. *Fino*, the driest of the sherries, is a light, golden aperitif that should be served chilled. A type of *fino* called *manzanilla* is slightly richer; Sanlúcar de Barrameda is especially good. *Amontillado*, usually medium dry, is a deeper gold in colour, and is heavier than a true *fino*. *Amoroso* is medium sweet, with an amber colour, and *oloroso* is still more full-bodied.

The itinerary opens with Jerez's impressive prehistoric past (look out for some 4000-year-old cylinder-shaped idols with starburst eyes from Cerro de las Vacas). Star exhibits in the Greek and Roman sections include a seventh-century BC Greek military helmet, Roman amphorae – many stamped with the maker's name – and, in the Visigothic section, a sarcophagus carved with vegetable, animal and human symbols. The museum has added an expanded Moorish section with some fine ceramics – look out for an exquisite caliphal bottle vase – and interesting displays of artefacts relating to daily life in this period. Another new section dealing with the Christian Middle Ages features an exquisite fifteenth-century alabaster relief carved in England, and depicting the Resurrection of Christ; this is one of a number of similar works found in the town and underlines the importance of trade – not only in wine – between Jerez and the British Isles in this era.

Real Escuela Andaluza del Arte Ecuestre

MAP PAGE 100
Avda. Duque de Abrantes s/n. Charge.
www.realescuela.org.

Evidence of Jerez's great enthusiasm for horses can be seen at the **Real Escuela Andaluza del Arte Ecuestre** (Royal Andalusian School of Equestrian Art), which offers the chance to watch these elegant creatures perform to music. Training, rehearsals (without music) and visits to the stables and museum take place on weekdays.

Real Escuela Andaluza del Arte Ecuestre

Tapas bars and restaurants

El Almacén

MAP PAGE 100
C/La Torre 2, just north of Pza. del Arenal.
680 448 232.

Atmospheric tapas bar installed in a former grocery store (*almacén*). Tapas and *raciones* include *patatas bravas* (potatoes with spicy sauce) as well as *tablas* (boards of cheese and cured meats to share), plus various vegetarian options. Make sure not to miss out on the *tarta de manzana templada con helado* (warm apple tart with ice cream) which can only be described as paradise on a plate. €€

Bar Juanito

MAP PAGE 100
C/Pescadería Vieja 8. 627 456 989.

In a small passage off the west side of Plaza del Arenal, this is one of the most celebrated tapas bars in town, with a menu as endless as the number of excellent *finos* on offer. Specials include *berza jerezana* (chickpea stew) and the *mariscos* of the coast. Its pleasant terrace restaurant serves a good-value *menú del día* (lunch only). €€€

La Carboná

MAP PAGE 100
C/San Francisco de Paula 2.
www.lacarbona.com.

Cavernous and wonderfully atmospheric mid-priced restaurant inside an old *bodega*, specializing in charcoal-grilled fish and meat and – in season – fresh tuna. Its *maridajes con vino de jerez* presents five courses, each accompanied by the appropriate wine. €€€

La Condesa

MAP PAGE 100
Pza. Rafael Rivero, C/Tornería 24.
956 326 700.

The esteemed restaurant of *Hotel Palacio Garvey* is an excellent place for a meal, especially on its attractive terrace. A three-course menu is recommended and often features *solomillo en salsa oloroso* (pork loin in sherry sauce). House specials include a tasty *salmorejo de remolacha con mojama y feta* (beetroot gazpacho with tuna and feta cheese). €€€€

Tabanco Plateros

MAP PAGE 100
C/Algarve 35. 956 104 458.

Highly popular *tabanco* slightly northeast of the Plaza del Arenal. There's a good and extensive wine list (including the classics of Jerez) or excellent tapped beer to accompany a lengthy tapas menu. Standouts are *salchichón* (salami), *sardinas ahumadas* (smoked sardines), *alcachofas con anchoas* (artichokes with anchovies). €€

Bodegas

Bodegas Sandeman

MAP PAGE 100
C/Pizarro 10. www.sandeman.com.

Near to the equestrian school, this *bodega* (wine producer) runs tours led by guides wearing the black cape and caballero hat of its trademark Don.

Bodegas Tradición

MAP PAGE 100
C/Cordobeses 3. www.bodegastradicion.es.

This spot is so fancy it even has its own exquisite private art collection featuring works by Goya, Velázquez, El Greco and Zurbarán; its tours and tastings are just as fine.

González Byass

MAP PAGE 100
C/Manuel Maria González 12.
www.gonzalezbyass.com.

The largest *bodega* in town, *González Byass* has a cellar, *La Concha*, located near the catedral and Alcázar, designed by none other than Gustave Eiffel – the mastermind behind Paris's Eiffel Tower.

Cádiz

Cádiz is among the oldest settlements in Spain, founded around 1100 BC by the Phoenicians and one of the country's principal ports ever since. Its greatest period, however, and the era from which the central part of town takes most of its present appearance, was the eighteenth century. Then, with the silting up of the river to Seville, the port enjoyed a virtual monopoly on the Spanish–American trade in gold and silver. The wealth poured in and up sprang the Catedral, grand mansions, public buildings, dockyards, warehouses and the smaller churches. Inner Cádiz, built on a peninsula-island, remains much as it must have looked in those days, with its elegant open squares, sailors' alleyways and high, turreted houses. Literally crumbling from the effect of the sea air on its soft limestone, it has a tremendous atmosphere – definitely in decline, but still full of mystique.

La Viña

MAP PAGE 106

On the western side of the peninsula is **La Viña**, a fishermen's quarter where locals can be seen collecting crabs by the causeway to the military islet of Castillo de San Sebastián. They moor their boats off Playa de la Caleta – the small beach that starred in the Bond movie, *Die Another Day* in which Cádiz doubled as Havana. Narrow streets lined by pastel-painted townhouses open out onto dappled plazas where patrons sit outside tapas bars slurping down

Cádiz, one of the oldest settlements in Spain

Tapas bars flank La Viña's colourful streets

grilled razor clams and glasses of *fino* sherry. This characterful enclave is the heart of Cádiz's vibrant Carnival culture (see box), with scenes of revelry bringing the neighbourhood to life.

Museo de Cádiz

MAP PAGE 106
Charge, free with EU passport. 856 105 023.
Further around the headland, the **Museo de Cádiz**, the province's most important museum, overlooks the leafy Plaza de Mina. It incorporates the **Museo de Arqueología** on the ground floor, which has many important finds and artefacts from the city's lengthy history, including two remarkable fifth-century BC Phoenician carved sarcophagi in white marble (one male, the other female), which are unique to the western Mediterranean.

The upper floor houses the interesting **Museo de Bellas Artes**. A highlight is the quite exceptional series of saints painted by Zurbarán, brought here from the Carthusian monastery at Jerez and one of only three such sets in the country (the others are in Seville and Guadalupe) preserved intact, or nearly so. With their sharply defined shadows and intense, introspective air, Zurbarán's saints are at once powerful and very Spanish – even the English figures such as monk and bishop Hugh of Lincoln, or the Carthusian John Houghton, martyred by Henry VIII when he

Carnival celebrations

The city's famous Carnival is held in February or March, when Cádiz hosts ten days of music and revelry. This is the most spectacular Carnival celebration in mainland Spain and includes costumed parades and a competition for troubadours singing satirical songs.

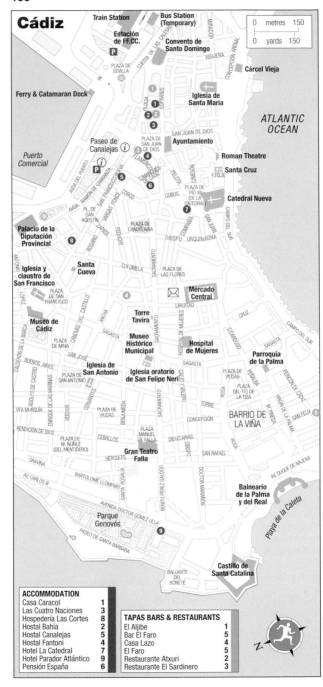

Cádiz

Train Station
Bus Station (Temporary)

Estación de FF.CC.

Convento de Santo Domingo

Ferry & Catamaran Dock

Iglesia de Santa María

Cárcel Vieja

ATLANTIC OCEAN

Puerto Comercial

Paseo de Canalejas

Ayuntamiento

Roman Theatre

Santa Cruz

Catedral Nueva

Palacio de la Diputación Provincial

Iglesia y claustro de San Francisco

Santa Cueva

Mercado Central

Torre Tavira

Museo de Cádiz

Museo Histórico Municipal

Hospital de Mujeres

Parroquia de la Palma

Iglesia de San Antonio

Iglesia oratorio de San Felipe Neri

BARRIO DE LA VIÑA

Gran Teatro Falla

Balneario de la Palma y del Real

Parque Genovés

Playa de la Caleta

Castillo de Santa Catalina

BALUARTE DEL BONETÉ

| 0 | metres | 150 |
| 0 | yards | 150 |

ACCOMMODATION

Casa Caracol	1
Las Cuatro Naciones	3
Hospedería Las Cortes	8
Hostal Bahía	2
Hostal Canalejas	5
Hostal Fantoni	4
Hotel La Catedral	7
Hotel Parador Atlántico	9
Pensión España	6

TAPAS BARS & RESTAURANTS

El Aljibe	1
Bar El Faro	5
Casa Lazo	4
El Faro	5
Restaurante Atxuri	2
Restaurante El Sardinero	3

Getting to Cádiz

Cádiz can be reached by train, bus or car. From Seville's Santa Justa station, it is a 1hr 45min train journey (17 daily; www. renfe.es) to reach Cádiz, whose station is on the periphery of the old town, close to Pza. de San Juan de Dios. By bus, the journey is the same amount of time though there are fewer services (8 daily). Coming by car (1hr 20min), you'll soon discover sea-locked Cádiz's acute lack of parking space, and if you don't want to spend an age searching you'd be best off taking accommodation with a garage (all the hotels will assist with parking) or heading for a car park – two of the most central inside the city walls are by the train station and along Paseo de Canalejas near the port.

refused to accept him as head of the English Church. Perhaps this is not surprising, for the artist spent much of his life travelling round the Carthusian monasteries of Spain and many of his saints are in fact portraits of the monks he met. Other important artists displayed here include Murillo, Ribera, Rubens and Alonso Cano.

Catedral Nueva

MAP PAGE 106
Charge.
Even if you don't normally go for High Baroque, it's hard to resist the attraction of the huge and crumbling eighteenth-century **Catedral Nueva**, so titled because it replaced the former cathedral, Santa Cruz. The building has undergone a ten-year (and astronomically expensive) restoration to preserve its interior, roof and "gilded" dome.

The Catedral's interior is decorated entirely in stone, with not a glimmer of gold in sight, and in absolutely perfect proportions. In the crypt, you can see the tomb of Manuel de Falla, the great *gaditano* (as inhabitants of Cádiz are known) composer of such Andalucía-inspired works as *Nights in the Gardens of Spain* and *El Amor Brujo*.

For a magnificent view over the city, climb the **Torre de Poniente**, one of the Catedral's twin towers.

Iglesia Santa Cruz

MAP PAGE 106
Free.
East of the Catedral on the edge of the Barrio del Pópulo, the city's oldest quarter dating from the Middle Ages, lies the "old" or original Catedral, **Santa Cruz**. This was one of the buildings severely knocked about by the Earl of Essex during the English assault on Cádiz in 1596, causing the thirteenth-century church to be substantially rebuilt. A fine Gothic entry portal survived, and inside there's a

Catedral Nueva

Mercado Central

magnificent seventeenth-century *retablo* with sculptures by Martínez Montañés. A first-century BC **Roman theatre** has been excavated behind, close to the sea.

Hospital de Mujeres

MAP PAGE 106
C/Hospital de Mujeres 26.
Charge; ask the porter for admission.

One of the most impressive Baroque buildings in the city, the chapel of the **Hospital de Mujeres**, houses a brilliant piece by **El Greco**, *St Francis in Ecstasy*. It's one of the Cretan artist's finest portrayals of the saint, although it's a rather sombre study using copious shades of grey.

Santa Cueva

MAP PAGE 106
C/Rosario s/n. Charge.

A short walk from the Museo de Cádiz is the eighteenth-century **Santa Cueva**, which houses three fine Goya frescoes. The church is divided into two dramatically contrasting parts. In the elliptical **upper oratory** beneath an elegant dome are three frescoes representing the *Miracle of the*

Loaves and Fishes, the *Bridal Feast* (either side of the main altar) and the *Last Supper* (above the entrance), an unexpected depiction of Christ and the disciples dining sprawled on the floor, Roman style. The other works here are depictions of biblical scenes by minor artists.

In sharp contrast to the chapel above is the **subterranean chapel**, containing a sculpture of the Crucifixion whose manifest pathos adds a sombre note. An eighteenth-century work of the Genoa school, the image is said to have inspired visiting composer Joseph Haydn to write his *Seven Last Words* (of Christ) oratorio. A small museum has been added between the two chapels giving background information on the building's history and includes a display of Haydn's original score.

Plaza de las Flores and Mercado Central

MAP PAGE 106

Head west from the Catedral and it's a couple of blocks to the **Plaza de las Flores** (aka Plaza Topete), one of the city's most emblematic squares. Fronted by the striking early twentieth-century *Correos*, the square is a riot of colour most days due to the many flower sellers that have their stalls here. Adjoining the plaza to the west is the Plaza de la Libertad, the whole of which is taken up by the nineteenth-century **Mercado Central**, an elegant Neoclassical construction with a colonnade of Doric pillars enclosing the central area. Following a five-year refurbishment, the building has been restored to its former glory. On weekday mornings it's a beehive of activity and not to be missed. In addition to the usual fish, meat, fruit and veg, the new-and-improved market has attracted a kaleidoscope of stalls selling everything from herbs and spices to teas and world beers as well as sushi and even fish and chips.

Tapas bars and restaurants

El Aljibe

MAP PAGE 106
C/Plocia 25. 956 266 656.

A very good restaurant serving up a range of traditional dishes. House specials include *frito gaditano* (fried fish) and *almejas a la marinera* (clams in garlic sauce); it also serves tasty tapas in its bar.

Bar El Faro

MAP PAGE 106
C/San Félix 15.
www.elfarodecadiz.com/la-barra.php.

Tapas bar of the renowned restaurant (see below), and probably the best in town. A stand-up place where the *finos* are first-rate, the service is slick and the seafood tapas are mouthwateringly delicious. House specials include *tortillitas de camarones* (shrimp fritters) and *tostaditas de pan con bacalao* (cod on toast).

Casa Lazo

MAP PAGE 106
C/Barrie 17, north of the market.
956 229 499.

Charming compact shop/bar with a tasty tapas and *raciones* selection. Try the *jamón, brochetas de pulpo* (octopus skewers) or *croquetas caseras* (croquettes). Also does meat dishes and has a good wine cellar.

El Faro

MAP PAGE 106
C/San Félix 15. www.elfarodecadiz.com.

In the heart of the La Viña, this is one of the best fish restaurants in Andalucía. House specialities include *pulpo* (octopus), *merluza* (hake), *urta* (sea bream), and a delicious *arroz marinero* (Andalusian paella). Its excellent tapas bar is also well worth a visit.

Restaurante Atxuri

MAP PAGE 106
C/Plocia 7. www.atxuri.es.

This is an outstanding and highly popular Basque fish restaurant where head chef Pedro Ladrón de Guevara has been impressing diners for forty years. His kitchen turns out delicious Basque- and *andaluz*-inspired fish dishes at reasonable prices. Also has an excellent tapas bar plating up meal-sized *media raciones*. You'd best book for the restaurant.

Restaurante El Sardinero

MAP PAGE 106
Pza. San Juan de Dios 5. 956 265 926.

Traditional *gaditano* fish restaurant with an all-day kitchen offering good-quality seafood dishes, which are served on a terrace facing the striking *ayuntamiento*.

Cádiz speciality *tortillitas de camarones* (shrimp fritters)

ACCOMMODATION

Pájaro Rebelde

Accommodation

Seville has some of the finest hotels in Andalucía. One of the most attractive areas to stay has traditionally been the Santa Cruz *barrio*, with its quaint accommodation, flora-filled courtyards and magical atmosphere. But other areas are now up to speed, the Centro Histórico included. Even up north towards the Alameda de Hércules, you'll find palatial stays off the beaten path; across the river in Triana, riverfront views and hidden boutique finds. The southern Sur area, near the Plaza de España and Parque de María Luisa, has less variety but there are some options if you're looking to take in views of the monument. If you're planning to visit Seville during any of the major festivals, particularly Semana Santa or the Feria de Abril (April Fair), book as far ahead as possible – be aware, also, that this is when hotel rates rise even above the high season rates quoted below.

Centro Histórico

LA BANDA ROOFTOP HOSTEL MAP PAGE 28, POCKET MAP D8. C/Dos de Mio 16. www.labandahostel.com. An artistic place that fosters community through the likes of shared "family" dinners (€8–10) and live music or DJs on the rooftop overlooking the Catedral. The four- to eight-bed dorms are clean and comfortable, and the kitchen is well equipped. It also offers private rooms. 24hr reception. €

LAS CASAS DEL REY DE BAEZA MAP PAGE 28, POCKET MAP F6. Pza. Jesús de la Redención 2. www.hospes.com. Wonderful hotel with rooms arranged around an eighteenth-century *sevillano*

corral. Stylishly furnished pastel-shaded rooms come with traditional exterior *esparto* blinds; the restaurant's setting in the courtyard is just as special, plus there's a rooftop pool to cool off in. €€€€

H10 CASA DE LA PLATA MAP PAGE 28, POCKET MAP E6. C/Lagar 2. www.h10hotels.com. Beautifully decorated spot in between Las Setas and Plaza del Salvador, with a light-filled interior patio and rooftop pool. Rooms are elegant with local touches, like hand-painted tiles. €€€€

HOTEL BOUTIQUE CASA DE COLÓN MAP PAGE 28, POCKET MAP E7. C/Hernando Colón 3. www.hotelcasade colon.com. A small boutique hotel set in

Accommodation price codes

Each accommodation reviewed in this Guide is accompanied by a price category, based on the cost of a standard double room in high season. Price ranges don't include breakfast, unless stated otherwise.

€	Under €60
€€	€60–120
€€€	€121–180
€€€€	Over €180

an eighteenth-century palace, right in the centre of the action. Rooms are cosy and airy, and breakfast (€11) is served on the outdoor terrace. €€€

HOTEL SIMÓN MAP PAGE 28, POCKET MAP D8. C/García de Vinuesa 19. www.hotelsimonsevilla.com. Well-restored mansion in an excellent position across from the Catedral, with parking nearby. All rooms are en suite and a/c, and bargain deals can be snapped up online. €€€

HOTEL ZAIDA MAP PAGE 28, POCKET MAP C6. C/San Roque 26. www.hotelzaida. com. This intimate budget hotel is in a delightful, restored eighteenth-century townhouse with an attractive Mudéjar-style courtyard and halls graced with Moorish arches. €€

OASIS BACKPACKERS HOSTEL MAP PAGE 28, POCKET MAP E6. C/Alimrante Ulloa 1 and C/Compañia 1. www.oasissevilla. com. With two locations in the centre of town, these clean and friendly hostels offer common co-working spaces, loads of nighttime activities, and fun rooftop hangouts. Bed linens are provided. €

SANTIAGO 15 CASA PALACIO MAP PAGE 28, POCKET MAP F6. C/Santiago 15. www.santiago.alojamientosconenconto sevilla.com. A newly renovated eighteenth-century palace with 28 tastefully decorated rooms and suites, many of which retain the original coloured-tile floors. The intimate nature makes it ideal for couples. €€

TOC HOSTEL MAP PAGE 28, POCKET MAP E9. C/Miguel Mañara 18–22. www.tochostels.com. So close to the Catedral that it almost sits in its shadow, *TOC* is a forward-thinking place. It has the efficiency of a hotel coupled with the open atmosphere of a hostel. The brilliance is in the detail: environmentally friendly automatic lighting and a fingerprint entry system. €

Santa Cruz

LA CASA DEL MAESTRO MAP PAGE 44, POCKET MAP F6. C/Niño Ricardo 5. www.lacasadelmaestro.com. The maestro

in question is Manuel Serrapi Sánchez, one of Seville's most acclaimed guitarists, who was born nearby in 1904 and later made this his home. It is off the main tourist beat but very close to the Casa de Pilatos and a comfortable walk from Santa Cruz. €€

LAS CASAS DE LA JUDERÍA MAP PAGE 44, POCKET MAP F8. C/Santa María La Blanca. www.lascasasdelajuderiasevilla.com. Take a step back in time to another century at this opulent hotel adorned with antiques, art pieces and a collection of furniture that will make feel like you're sleeping among royals. The intriguing entrance is right next door to the Iglesia de Santa María la Blanca. Take the time to indulge in the Termas de Hispalis Roman bath experience. €€€€

EL CICERONE DE SEVILLA MAP PAGE 44, POCKET MAP F8. C/Mesón del Moro 10. www.cicerone.alojamientosconenconto sevilla.com. A small boutique bolthole whose nineteenth-century building was designed by the architect Aníbal González (he was also behind the Plaza de España). Rooms are newly renovated and pristinely clean, and family rooms come with bunks and twin heds. €€

HALO BOUTIQUE HOTEL SEVILLA MAP PAGE 44, POCKET MAP F8. C/Gloria 3. www.hotelhalodesevilla.com. Set in the heart of Santa Cruz, *Halo* is a chic boutique hotel with soundproof windows, plush beds and top-notch service. Spa services are also available. €€€€

HOSTAL PUERTA CARMONA MAP PAGE 44, POCKET MAP G7. Pza. de San Agustín 5. www.hostalpuertacarmona. com. Pleasant *hostal* on the edge of Santa Cruz, with indoor and outdoor patios. The good-value en-suite rooms come with a/c and TV. €€

HOTEL AMADEUS MAP PAGE 44, POCKET MAP F7. C/Farnesio 6. www.hotelamadeussevilla.com. Welcoming hotel housed in an eighteenth-century *casa señorial* where there's a *sala de música*, a grand piano on the patio and a variety of musical instruments to borrow. The stylish rooms come with thoughtful touches: soundproofing, a/c, robes and organic amenities. It's topped off with a stunning roof terrace (with telescope and whirlpool) for coffee or cocktails. €€€

HOTEL MURILLO MAP PAGE 44, POCKET MAP F8. C/Lope de Rueda 7. www.hotelmurillo.com. Traditional hotel in a restored mansion close to Plaza Santa Cruz with amusingly kitsch features, including suits of armour and paint-palette keyrings. Also rents out fully equipped apartments nearby. €€

PENSIÓN PÉREZ MONTILLA MAP PAGE 44, POCKET MAP G8. Pza. de los Curtidores 13. www.pensionperezmontilla. com. Spotless, budget-friendly *hostal* situated on a tranquil square. The cheaper options come without a private bathroom; en-suite rooms have a/c, heating and TV. Ask for an exterior room as these have more light. €

SANTACRUZ HOSTAL PLAZA MAP PAGE 44, POCKET MAP F8. C/Santa Teresa 15. www.santacruz.alojamientosconencanto sevilla.com. An elegant *sevillano* facade and a tranquil stay down from the Plaza Santa Cruz; a snip considering the prime location. Each luminous room is equipped with a/c and TV; some are located in a separate building. €€

Sur

HOTEL ALCÁZAR MAP PAGE 52, POCKET MAP F9. Avda. Menéndez Pelayo 10. www.hotelalcazar.com. Set behind the Plaza de España, *Hotel Alcázar* offers simple but comfortable rooms, with wooden floors. Snag a room with a balcony and gaze out over the plaza before heading out to explore. €€

HOTEL ALFONSO XIII MAP PAGE 52, POCKET MAP E9, E10. C/San Fernando 2. www.hotel-alfonsoxiii-seville. com. Expect old-style elegance in this renovated luxury hotel, built in neo-Mudéjar style in the 1920s commissioned by the King of Spain to play host to international dignitaries during the '29 Expo. A splendid patio, sleek and stylish

guest rooms, and a string of gastronomic and poolside restaurants. €€€€

HOTEL PASARELA MAP PAGE 52, POCKET MAP G11. Avda. de la Borbolla 11. www.hotelpasarela.com. In the backyard of Plaza de España (it's the closest hotel to the monument), with sensible no-frills interiors. Despite its proximity to the centre, it's a world away from the bustling streets of downtown and has easy access to Parque de María Luisa. €€

MELIÁ SEVILLA MAP PAGE 52, POCKET MAP G11. C/Dr. Pedro de Castro 1. www.melia.com. A stone's throw from the Plaza de España, this Spanish brand feels surprisingly cheerful for a corporate hotel, with its collection of modern, refurbished rooms. Take in views of the monument from the large swimming pool area. €€€

Triana and the Guadalquivir

CAVALTA BOUTIQUE HOTEL MAP PAGE 58, POCKET MAP A9. C/San Jacinto 89. www.cavaltaboutiquehotel.com. Deep into the Triana neighbourhood and away from the buzz, this stylishly designed new spot has just twelve luxury rooms and suites. Breakfast is included, and there's a rooftop garden club and pool area for soaking up the sun. €€€€

EUROSTARS GUADALQUIVIR MAP PAGE 58, POCKET MAP C11. Avda. de la República Argentina 23. www.eurostarshotels.com. Across the river from Puerta de Jerez in the residential area of Los Remedios, which neighbours Triana; you're only a ten-minute walk from the centre of Seville. While a bit outdated on the outside, the interiors are fresh, with all the comforts of a new big-brand hotel. Breakfast included. €€€

HOTEL RIBERA DE TRIANA MAP PAGE 58, POCKET MAP A7. Pza. de Chapina. www.hotelriberadetriana.com. A riverfront hotel with comfortable rooms, many with views of the Guadalquivir. And if not, the gym, swimming pool and hot tub all boast sweeping river vistas. €€€

EL NARANJITO DE TRIANA MAP PAGE 58, POCKET MAP A7. C/Pagés de Coro 5. 610 054 578. A small holiday apartment complex with a swimming pool and spacious airy rooms with minimalist interiors. Each apartment has a fully equipped kitchen, and even the one-bedroom units have sofa beds for extra travellers. Keep in mind there is usually two-night minimum stay. €€€

NOCHES EN TRIANA MAP PAGE 58, POCKET MAP A8. C/Pagés de Coro 51. www.nochesentriana.com. The canary-yellow central fountain and original exposed wooden beams give this cozy hotel its *trianera* charm. Rooms are simple and straightforward, each with 1V and a/c. €€

TRIANA BACKPACKERS HOSTEL MAP PAGE 58, POCKET MAP C9. C/Rodrigo de Triana 69. www.trianahostel.com. A simple hostel with 24hr reception and a rooftop whirlpool. Bed sheets and breakfast are included in the price. €

TRIANA BOUTIQUE APARTMENTS MAP PAGE 58, POCKET MAP A8. C/Alfarería 49. 854 529 775. Stay in your very own *corral de vecinos* in these affordable, fully equipped apartments in the heart of Triana. They're smartly designed and maintain many of the original features, like the dark wooden beams, iron balconies and interior fountain. €€

ZENIT SEVILLA MAP PAGE 58, POCKET MAP B9. C/Pagés de Corro 90B. www.sevilla.zenithoteles.com. A larger modern hotel with an excellent rooftop pool; just a short walk to the river. Family rooms are ideal for larger groups, and you can also rent out recently renovated apartments for extra space and comfort. Underground parking available. €€€

Alameda

H10 CORREGIDOR BOUTIQUE HOTEL MAP PAGE 66, POCKET MAP E5. C/Amor de Dios 34. www.h10hotels.com. A smart boutique hotel a few blocks from the Alameda de Hércules means you can dip into the city's nightlife, without the noise. Highlights include the excellent breakfast (not included), served on a pretty patio, and the rooftop plunge pool. €€€

CASA ROMANA HOTEL BOUTIQUE MAP PAGE 66, POCKET MAP D5. C/Trajano 15. www.hotelcasaromana.com. Spread across a pair of connecting palatial homes, this sleek hotel is located between Las Setas and the Alameda neighbourhood, with reasonable prices for its four-star rating. The interior patio has stunning tilework and the lively rooftop bar, *Roof*, is one of the best in the city. €€

THE CORNER HOUSE MAP PAGE 66, POCKET MAP D4. Alamede de Hércules 11. www.thecornerhousesevilla.com. Twelve rooms, each with its own funky touch, right in the centre of the bustling Alameda de Hércules. The restaurant below, *El Disparate*, is one of the best on the plaza and the pride of the hotel. €€€

EXE SEVILLA MACARENA MAP PAGE 66, POCKET MAP F2. San Juan de Ribera 2. www.eurostarshotels.com. Across from the Basílica de la Macarena, this 331-room hotel with grand ballrooms belongs to the Eurostars brand. There's a large swimming pool and sun deck, and a breakfast buffet is included in the stay. €€

HOTEL SACRISTÍA DE SANTA ANA MAP PAGE 66, POCKET MAP D4. Alameda de Hércules 22. www.hotelsacristia.com. Beautiful hotel with delightful classically decorated rooms – the external ones have Alameda views – inside a seventeenth-century *casa señorial* with many original features. Reserve direct on the hotel website for better prices and a late checkout. €€

JARDIN DE LA ALAMEDA BOUTIQUE MAP PAGE 66, POCKET MAP E3. Jesús del Gran Poder 130. www.jardinalameda. alojamientosconencantosevilla.com. A small and cutesy corner hotel at the edge of the Alameda de Hércules with a relaxing rooftop terrace. Rooms are neat, clean and affordable and come with a/c, TV and toiletries. €€

PÁJARO REBELDE MAP PAGE 66, POCKET MAP D4. C/Martínez Montañés 27. www.elpajarorebelde.com. Tucked away on a quiet street in San Lorenzo, this boutique hotel is run by a delightful French couple who also live on the premises. Each room is full of unique touches, with design elements specially curated by the owners. The orange trees in the beautiful interior patio provide a tranquil spot for lounging by the pool or sipping drinks. The fabulous breakfast spread is included. €€€€

PATIO DE ALAMEDA MAP PAGE 66, POCKET MAP E3. Alameda de Hércules 31. www.patiodelaalameda.com. Bright, modern and pleasant *hostal* overlooking the tree-lined Alameda de Hércules, with a relaxing rooftop terrace. En-suite rooms are all exterior-facing with small balconies and come with a/c and TV. €€€

Ronda

ALAVERA DE LOS BAÑOS C/Molino de Alarcón s/n. www.alaveradelosbanos.com. Enchanting small hotel with stylish rooms (some with terraces), garden and swimming pool. Pick one of the guest rooms to the rear for views of sheep-speckled hills across the river. It also has a couple of elegant suites. €€€

CAMPING EL SUR Carretera Ronda–Algeciras Km2.8. www.campingelsur. com. Ronda's campsite with pool, bar and restaurant lies some 3km out of town along the Algeciras road (A369). Tent pitches €, apartments €€€€

HOTEL ANDALUCÍA C/Martínez Astein 19. www.hotel-andalucia.net. Pleasant en-suite rooms in leafy surroundings opposite the train station. €

HOTEL COLÓN C/Pozo 1. www.hcolon.es. Charming small hotel with a/c en-suite rooms; the best ones open onto a spacious roof terrace. €€

HOTEL SOHO BOUTIQUE PALACIO SAN GABRIEL C/Marqués de Moctezuma 19. www.sohoteles.com. A lovely boutique hotel housed in a beautifully restored eighteenth-century mansion. It offers 22 guest rooms furnished with original antiques, a library, cosy wine cellar and an amusing five-seater cinema for guests. €€

PARADOR DE RONDA Pza. de España. www.paradores.es. Ronda's imposing parador offers elegantly furnished rooms with spectacular views overlooking El Tajo, plus a swimming pool, terrace bar and excellent restaurant. €€€€

Grazalema

CASA DE LAS PIEDRAS C/Las Piedras 6. www.casadelaspiedras.es. The only budget option, this friendly family-run *hostal* is located above the main square. It offers comfortable en-suite rooms and also rents out some apartments nearby. The *hostal's* restaurant, with a vine-covered patio for alfresco dining, serves local dishes with a creative edge. €

HOTEL VILLA DE GRAZALEMA Finca El Olivar s/n. www.villasdeandalucia. com. This three-star hotel lies in leafy surroundings on the village's northern edge (a 3min walk) and has comfortable rooms with terrace balconies and fine views. Facilities include a restaurant and bar, pool and free parking; also rents out cottages sleeping up to four. Doubles €, cottages €€

LA MEJORANA C/Santa Clara 6. www.lamejorana.net. One of the most attractive places to stay in the village, this welcoming *hostal* offers comfortably furnished rooms (many with views) in an elegant *casa señorial* complete with pool. Minimum booking of two nights during high season. €

Ubrique

HOTEL OCURRIS Avda. Dr Solís Pascual 49. www.hotelocurris.com. This two-star hotel on the main street has pleasant enough en-suite rooms with a/c and TV, plus its own tapas bar and restaurant. €€

Aracena

CAMPING EL MADROÑAL 1km out of Fuenteheridos, along the HU8114 towards Castaño Robledo. www.campingelmadronal.com. Welcoming campsite with mature trees providing plenty of shade, and with decent facilities, including a large pool and restaurant. Tents €, bungalows €€

HOSPEDERÍA REINA DE LOS ÁNGELES
Avda. Reina de los Ángeles s/n, near the Gruta de las Maravillas. 959 128 367. A rather institutional-looking place that betrays its origins as a former student hostel. However, redecorated and refitted, its ninety en-suite and rather spartan rooms are nevertheless clean, bright and good value. Easy street parking. €

HOTEL CONVENTO ARACENA C/Jesús
María 19. www.hotelconventoaracena. es. The town's four-star luxury option is located inside a tastefully restored sixteenth- to eighteenth-century former Dominican convent. Rooms overlook the cloisters and quadrangle, now planted with trees and aromatic herbs. Facilities include a spa and pool with a view over the mountains. A former convent herb garden now stands outside the hotel's top-notch restaurant, *Huerto*. €€€

HOTEL SIERRA DE ARACENA Gran Vía
21. www.hotelsierradearacena.com. This traditional hotel has pleasant, decent-sized rooms, half of which have views of the castle. €€

Carmona
HOSTAL COMERCIO C/Torre del Oro 56.
954 140 018. Built into the Puerta de Sevilla gateway, this charming small and friendly family-run *hostal* celebrated its centenary in 2014. It offers compact a/c en-suite rooms (without TV) around a pretty patio, some with views of the church. €

HOTEL SAN PEDRO C/San Pedro 1.
954 141 606. Near the Iglesia de San Pedro, this central and pleasant budget option has a/c en-suite rooms with TV. Below, there's a café that serves a decent breakfast. €

PARADOR DE CARMONA Alcázar Rey Don
Pedro. www.parador.es. Despite more recent competition at this end of the market, a superb location, patios and swimming pool ensure that this is still the nicest – and best value – of the luxury places in town. Pay a few euro extra for a room with a balcony. It's

worth calling in for a drink at the bar, to enjoy the fabulous views from the terrace. €€€€

Córdoba
ALBERGUE JUVENIL MAP PAGE 88.
Pza. de Judá Levi. www.inturjoven. com. Excellent and superbly located modern youth hostel (with twin, triple and four-person en-suite rooms). It's a prime destination for budget travellers, so you may need to book ahead at busy periods. €€

CAMPAMENTO MUNICIPAL EL BRILLANTE
MAP PAGE 88. Avda. El Brillante 50. www.campingelbrillante.com. Córdoba's local campsite (with restaurant and pool) is around 2km north of the centre in the El Brillante barrio, and served by bus #10 or #11 from the bus station. Tents and equipment for hire. €

CASA DE LOS AZULEJOS MAP
PAGE 88. C/Fernando Colón 5. www.casadelosazulejos.com. Stylish, small boutique B&B with distinctively furnished rooms, featuring iron bedsteads and artworks, ranged around a leafy patio, itself used for art shows. Also has pool and own car park. €€

HOSTAL ALCÁZAR MAP PAGE 88.
C/San Basilio 2. www.hostalalcazar.com. Comfortable and welcoming family-run B&B *hostal* with a nice patio and a range of en-suite rooms with a/c and TV. Also has some good-value apartments opposite (sleeping up to four people; €80), and its own car park. €

HOSTAL ALMANZOR MAP PAGE
88. Corregidor Luís de la Cerda 10. www.hostal–almanzor.es. East of the Mezquita, a pleasant refurbished *hostal*, with a/c, en-suite rooms with TV. Free use of car park. €€

HOSTAL & HOTEL MAESTRE MAP
PAGE 88. C/Romero Barros 4 & 16. www.hotelmaestre.com. Excellent *hostal*, between C/San Fernando and the Plaza del Potro, and neighbouring hotel with attractive a/c en-suite rooms with TV. Also has some good-value two-person apartments. €€

HOTEL AMISTAD CÓRDOBA MAP PAGE 88. Pza. de Maimónides 3. www.nh-hoteles.com. Stylish upmarket hotel with comfortable rooms incorporating three eighteenth-century mansions, near the old wall in La Judería. Car park available. €€€

HOTEL BALCÓN DE CÓRDOBA MAP PAGE 88. C/Encarnación 8. www.balcondecordoba.com. Luxurious boutique hotel in a restored seventeenth-century convent. Features include plenty of original elements, a patio restaurant, rooftop terrace with close-up views of the Mezquita, and comfy, spacious rooms. Breakfast included. Parking can be arranged nearby. €€€€

HOTEL LAS CASAS DE LA JUDERÍA MAP PAGE 88. C/Tomás Conde 10. www.casasypalacios.com. This four-star hotel is an exquisitely charming restoration of an ancient *casa palacio* and rooms are arranged around patios with tinkling fountains and scented flowers. The elegant rooms are decorated with period furnishings and artworks and come with TV and lots of frills. Also has a spa, restaurant and garage. €€€€

HOTEL MEZQUITA MAP PAGE 88. Pza. Santa Catalina 1. www.hotelmezquita.com. Atmospheric and central hotel in a converted sixteenth-century mansion with excellent a/c rooms. €€€

LA LLAVE DE LA JUDERÍA MAP PAGE 88. C/Romero 38. www.lallavedelajuderia.es. Elegant and welcoming nine-room hotel in La Judería. Entry is through a double patio, and rooms are classically furnished with chintz drapes and bedcovers, and some have terraces. Facilities include minibar, in-room internet and rooftop terrace. €€€

PARADOR DE CÓRDOBA MAP PAGE 88. Avda. de la Arruzafa s/n, off Avda. El Brillante. www.parador.es. Córdoba's modern parador is located on the outskirts of the city 5km to the north of the Mezquita, but compensates with pleasant gardens, a pool and every other amenity (including a shooting range). €€€€

PENSIÓN EL PORTILLO MAP PAGE 88. C/Cabezas 2. www.pensionelportillo.com. Beautiful, refurbished and friendly old *hostal* with elegant patio, offering en-suite a/c singles and doubles. €€

SÉNECA HOSTAL MAP PAGE 88. C/Conde y Luque 7. www.senecahostel.com. Wonderful place to stay, with simple en-suite rooms around a stunning patio with Moorish pavement where you can take breakfast. Very popular, so book as far ahead as possible. €€

Jerez de la Frontera

ALBERGUE JUVENIL MAP PAGE 100. Avda. Blas Infante 30. 856 814 001. Good-value seven-storey hostel with double a/c en-suite rooms and a swimming pool; but out in the suburbs. Take bus #9 from outside the bus station. €

HOTEL AL ANDALUS MAP PAGE 100. C/Arcos 29. www.hotelalandalusjerez.es. Comfortable hotel with two pretty patios. Individually styled rooms come with bold colour schemes and the better ones – off the inner patio – are equipped with a/c and TV. €

HOTEL BELLAS ARTES MAP PAGE 100. Pza. del Arroyo 45, facing the Catedral. www.hotelbellasartes.net. Charming and good-value small hotel inside a refurbished *casa palacio* on the Catedral square. Individually styled rooms are well equipped with minibar and plasma TV, and the public areas include a library and roof terrace (with loungers) for having breakfast or enjoying a fine view of the Catedral and surrounding town. Also has a couple of suites. €€

HOTEL DOÑA BLANCA MAP PAGE 100. C/Bodegas 11. www.hoteldonablanca.com. One of the most central and intimate of the upper-range places, with well-equipped a/c balcony rooms with minibar and TV, on a quiet street. Own garage. €€

HOTEL-HOSTAL SAN ANDRÉS MAP PAGE 100. C/Morenos 12. www.hotelypensionsanandres.com. Excellent and friendly spot offering (in the *hostal*) both en-suite rooms, and those sharing bath; the hotel's rooms are all en suite with a/c and TV. There's also a charming patio below. €

PENSIÓN LAS PALOMAS MAP PAGE 100. C/Higueras 17. www.pension-las-palomas. es. The most central budget option, with clean and simple rooms, some en suite. €

Cádiz

CASA CARACOL MAP PAGE 106. C/Suárez de Salazar 4. www.casacaracolcadiz.com. Friendly backpackers' place with dorm beds in a large house near Plaza de San Juan de Dios; also has some double rooms sharing bathrooms and pricier en-suite rooms in a new *hostal* nearby. Note that room prices rise significantly on Fri & Sat nights. Breakfast is included, guests have use of a communal kitchen, and the proprietors hire out cycles and surfboards. €

LAS CUATRO NACIONES MAP PAGE 106. C/Plocia 3. www.lascuatronaciones.es. A stone's throw from Plaza de San Juan de Dios and close to the train and bus stations, this is a clean, unpretentious place with low-priced rooms sharing bathrooms. €

HOSPEDERÍA LAS CORTES MAP PAGE 106. C/San Francisco 9. www.hotellascortes.com. Splendid B&B hotel in a stylishly restored *casa señorial*. Elegant rooms are well equipped and include a minibar. Facilities include sauna and gym, and there's a cafetería and restaurant. High-season price August only. €€€

HOSTAL BAHÍA MAP PAGE 106. C/Plocia 5. www.hostalbahiacadiz.com. Reasonable-value and conveniently located hostal, offering a/c rooms with baths. Request one of the more attractive balcony rooms. Pay car park nearby. €€

HOSTAL CANALEJAS MAP PAGE 106. C/Cristóbal Colón 5. www.hostalcanalejas. com. Pleasant two-star *hostal* in completely restored townhouse. En-suite rooms come with a/c and TV, and there's a wi-fi zone plus car park nearby. Avoid the windowless interior rooms, though. €€

PENSIÓN ESPAÑA MAP PAGE 106. C/Marqués de Cádiz 9. www.pensionespana. com. Pleasant *hostal* inside a restored *casa palacio* offering reasonable en-suite rooms with fans (some sharing bath) ranged around a patio. €€

HOSTAL FANTONI MAP PAGE 106. C/Flamenco 5. www.hostalfantoni. es. Good-value *hostal* in a renovated townhouse with lots of *azulejos* and cool marble, offering simple and en-suite rooms, the latter with a/c and TV. €€

HOTEL LA CATEDRAL MAP PAGE 106. Pza. de la Catedral 9. www.hotellacatedral. com. Charming new small B&B hotel 50m from the Catedral's front door. Comfortable rooms are well equipped and many have balconies where you can feast your eyes on the Catedral's imposing facade. Add an infinity rooftop pool – where you seem to swim almost within touching distance of the Catedral's bell tower – and you have a perfect place to stay. Ring reception for the best available rate. €€€

HOTEL PARADOR ATLÁNTICO MAP PAGE 106. Parque Genovés 9. www.parador.es. This state-of-the-art rectilinear construction fronting the sea replaced the old parador which was razed to make way for it. Beyond an austere exterior – combining wood and rusting metal with stone and glass – lie 124 rooms and suites filled with five-star comforts, all with terrace balcony and sea view. Features include full-size rooftop swimming pool, solarium, bars, restaurant and gardens. €€€€

ESSENTIALS

Santa Justa train station

Arrival

By plane

Seville's airport lies 12km northeast of town along the A4 (NIV) *autovía* towards Córdoba. The airport bus (daily, roughly every 20min 5am–1am; €4 or €6 return), takes 45min to the centre and terminates at the central Plaza de Armas bus station, stopping at the train station en route. A taxi from the rank in front of the airport will cost €20–25; or book in advance with Book Taxi Sevilla (typically for a twenty percent mark-up; www.booktaxisevilla.com). You can also book ride shares like Uber or Spain's version, Cabify.

By train

Santa Justa train station is 5km northeast of the city on Avenida Kansas City, the airport road. Bus #32 will take you from here to Plaza del Duque de la Victoria, from where all sights are within easy walking distance; alternatively, bus #C1 will take you to the Prado de San Sebastián bus station. For train timetables and information, consult RENFE (www. renfe.es) or the new lower-cost Iryo (www.iryo.eu). Alternatively, visit the RENFE or Iryo office in the train station, where you can buy advanced tickets in person. There are regular RENFE services to Seville from all the major Spanish cities, including Barcelona (12 daily; 5hr 40min–7hr), Cádiz (16 daily; 1hr 45min), Córdoba (36 daily, 45min–1hr 20min), Granada (7 daily; 2hr 30min–3hr 50 min), Huelva (3 daily; 1hr 30min), Madrid (AVE 15 daily; 2hr 30min–3hr 20min) and Málaga (12 daily; 2–3hr). Iryo currently connects Seville to Córdoba (6 daily; 45min) and Madrid (6 daily, 2hr 30min).

By bus

Plaza de Armas bus station is on the square of the same name, by the Puente del Cachorro on the river. Buses from this station are operated by Alsa (www.alsa.es), which covers long-distance national and international destinations; and Damas (www.damas-sa.es), which is the most prominent provider for longer routes within Andalucía. For the majority of coaches, you'll have an allocated seat. Prado de San Sebastián, the city's subsidiary bus station, is on Avenida Carlos V, which runs along the north edge of Jardines del Prado de San Sebastián. Both Alsa and Damas providers call here. Some buses occasionally also leave from the Santa Justa station.

By car

Driving in Seville is an ordeal, especially in the narrow streets of *barrios* such as Santa Cruz, which is supposed to be pedestrianized. As on-street parking spaces are almost impossible to find, your best bet for parking is to find a pay car park (they are signed all around the central zone), or to choose accommodation with a garage (for which you will be charged extra).

Getting around

Though it's the fourth largest city in the country, Seville feels relatively small in comparison to other major Spanish cities, and it is best explored on foot. Not only is walking faster than other modes of transport (narrow one-ways aren't great for traffic; buses aren't exceptionally efficient; and the metro is best suited for reaching the suburbs), but it is also the best way to get a feel for the city and discover all its hidden corners. If you're travelling in the sweltering summer months or just need to rest your feet, the tram (*tranvía*) is a relaxing way to travel from one monument-concentrated part of the city to another.

Bus

All inner-city bus journeys have a flat fare of €1.40 (cash only). Seville's bus and tram company, Tussam (www.tussam.es), also sells one-day (€5) or three-day (€10) *tarjetas turísticas* for unlimited journeys, with a €1.50 card deposit. These are available from the Tussam offices at Prado San Sebastián, Plaza Ponce de León station, Avenida Andalucía 11 (one of the two local bus hubs with Puerta de Jerez), or at the Santa Justa train station.

If you're staying for longer, it's worth buying a *tarjeta multiviaje* rechargeable card from a kiosk (also good for trams). The first load-up will cost you €8.50 (€7 minimum spend; €1.50 card deposit) but, after that, journeys are just €0.69 or €0.76. A bus map detailing routes is available from the tourist office, or download the Tussam app on your phone.

Trams

The *tranvía* city tram runs from Plaza Nueva to San Bernardo bus station, stopping at Archivo de Indias, San Fernando and Prado de San Sebastián along the way. A single journey costs €1.40, and you buy tickets at the tram stops (you can also use the *tarjeta multiviaje* rechargeable card on board).

Metro

Seville currently has just one, 18km-long metro line (three more are planned), connecting the suburbs beyond Triana with Montequinto to the east. It's air-conditioned – convenient if you arrive at San Bernardo in the heat of the day and are staying close to, or over, the river. Otherwise, you likely won't need to use it. A single zone ticket is €1.35.

Open-top bus tour

Good for time-strapped visitors, this hop-on-hop-off service is operated by City Sightseeing Sevilla (www.city-sightseeing.com); buses leave half-hourly from Torre del Oro, stopping at or near the main sites (24hr ticket €27, 48hr €33; half-price for kids). Headset commentary is available in sixteen languages.

Taxis and rideshares

The main central ranks are in Plaza Nueva, Plaza Duque de la Victoria, the Alameda de Hércules and the Plaza de Armas and Prado de San Sebastián bus stations. The basic charge for a short journey is around €7 but rates increase at night and over the weekend. For a reliable taxi pick-up, try Radio Taxi (954 580 000). Uber is also available in the city, as well as the local version Cabify. Both tend to have similar rates.

Bike

Joint winner of the European Capital of Smart Tourism for 2023, Seville is championing sustainable travel – and greener transport is just one of its eco-conscious pushes. The city is flat and pleasant to cycle, with plenty of green spaces and 180km of bike lanes. The Parque de María Luisa, with its fountains and gazebos, is a scenic spot to peddle – or just outside the city centre is Alamillo Park on the Isla de la Cartuja. Sevici bike depots are dotted throughout the city, costing €13 for unlimited access for a week. The first thirty minutes are free, and you'll pay €1 for the first extra hour and €2 for every following hour. Alternatively, lots of private companies offer rentals for around €15/day.

Directory A–Z

Accessible travel

Accessible Travel Press has a full Seville Accessibility Guide available online for free. https://accessible travel.online/wp-content/uploads/2020/05/Sevilla-Accessibility-Guide-1_compressed.pdf.

Addresses

The street name is always written before the building number in Seville addresses. The floor numbers start with zero, meaning the ground floor is in fact 0 and the second floor is then 1 or "primero".

Children

Though walking and cobblestone streets aren't an ideal mix for children and babies, that doesn't stop anyone. Seville is very kid-friendly, and you'll see plazas swarming with children kicking around football balls, families pushing strollers in every part of town, and the most important local invention: playgrounds surrounded by tapas bars where parents can safely watch their little ones while enjoying some adult time.

Cinema

Cinema tickets are relatively inexpensive in Seville. The Avenida 5 Cine near Plaza de Armas (C/Marqués de Paradas 15) shows films in their original language (the majority of movies in Spain are dubbed) and will only set you back around €7.50 or €5 on Wednesdays.

Crime and emergencies

Central local police stations are at the north end of the Alameda de Hércules and in Triana at Calle Santa Fe 1. Dial 092 or 112 (local police) or 091 (national) in an emergency.

Electricity

The standard continental 220 volts AC. Most European appliances should work as long as you have an adaptor for continental-style two-pin round plugs. North Americans will need this plus a transformer. It is not recommended to bring certain appliances like hairdryers or curling irons, as the conversion and volt difference can destroy the device.

Embassies and consulates

Ireland consulate Avenida de Jerez 21, 954 690 689.
UK consulate Calle Américo Vespucio 5, 952 352 300.
US consulate Plaza Nueva 8B, Planta 2, 954 218 751.

Health

Clínica Santa Isabel (private; C/Luis Montoto 100) and Quiron Salud Sagrado Corazón (C/Rafael Salgado 3) offer English-language medical services. English-speaking doctors are usually available at Hospital Universitario Virgen Macarena (public), Calle Dr Marañon s/n (955 008 000), behind the Andalucía parliament building to the north of the centre. For emergencies, dial 061. Hospital Macarena and Hospital Virgen del Rocío, along with many public clinics around town, also offer telephone interpreter services in English.

Also, 24hr pharmacies can be found at: Calle Amador de los Rios 31, Avenida de Menéndez Pelayo 12 and República Argentina 10.

Internet

The vast majority of hotels and cafés have free wi-fi, and there's complimentary wi-fi access at the airport, Plaza de Armas bus station and Santa Justa train station.

Left luggage

There are coin-operated lockers (ask for the *consigna*) located at the Santa Justa train station (6am–12.30am), and left-luggage offices situated at the Prado de San Sebastián (24hr) and Plaza de Armas (open during station hours) bus stations.

LGBTQ+

Spain is a very LGBTQ-friendly country. Despite living under an oppressive conservative dictatorship up until 1975, the country has done a relative 180 in terms of its social progression: Spain was one of the first countries in the world to legalize same-sex marriage, in 2005. The Alameda neighbourhood has the highest concentration of LGBTQ+ bars and clubs.

Lost property

Oficina de Objetos Perdidos, Calle Otto Engelhardt 3, next to the Prado de San Sebastián bus station (Mon–Fri 8.30am–2.15pm; 955 472 277).

Money

Bureaux de change can be found on Avenida de la Constitución, around the Catedral, and on Calle Tetuán. ATMs can be found all over the city, though most places take card.

Opening hours

Most shops, other than big box stores, open around 10am and close in the middle of the day for siesta, around 2pm. They'll usually open up again around 5pm and close at 9pm. Museums and monuments tend to stay open all day.

Phones

Most mobile phones from the EU can now be used in Spain as at home with no roaming charges. For countries outside the EU, you will need to speak with your mobile phone provider to find the best rates. The area code for Spain is +34.

Post offices

Avenida de la Constitución 32, by the Catedral; *Lista de Correos* (poste restante) Mon–Fri 8.30am–8.30pm, Sat 9.30am–1pm. The office is closed on the weekends.

Price codes

Accommodation and restaurant listings throughout this Guide are accompanied by a corresponding price code; see boxes on page 112 and below.

Smoking

Smoking and vaping are not permitted indoors, but that doesn't inhibit people from lighting up on the street or right next to you on a restaurant patio.

Time

The Spanish peninsula (not including the Canary Islands) is on Central European Time (CET), one hour ahead of Britain and six hours ahead of EST, with the clocks going forward in spring

Eating out price codes

Each restaurant and tapas bars reviewed in this Guide is accompanied by a price category, based on the cost of a two-course meal (or similar) for one, including a soft drink.

€	Under €20
€€	€20–40
€€€	€41–80
€€€€	over €80

and back again some time in autumn – the exact date changes from year to year. Generally speaking, Spaniards use the 24hr clock.

Tipping

Tipping is discretionary and not expected. For taxis, you can round up the fare to the nearest euro. You can tip bellhops at the hotel or leave a few euros for housekeeping. At restaurants it's not necessary, though rounding up or leaving a few euros never hurts, especially if the service is good. Do, however, tip any tour guides – about fifteen to twenty percent is customary.

Toilets

Public toilets are few and far between, save if you're in Parque de María Luisa or inside a monument or museum. You can, however, find them in many underground parking garages. Standards of hygiene can be low,

though they've improved drastically since the pandemic. Most locals carry around a pack of tissues in case there is no toilet paper.

Tourist information

Plaza del Triunfo 1, close to the exit from the Alcázar (Mon–Fri 9am–7.30pm, Sat & Sun 9.30am–7.30pm; 954 210 005). This office tends to be overwhelmed in peak periods, but it has accommodation lists and can give you a copy of the very useful free listings magazine *El Giraldillo*. Another, less chaotic *turismo* office is inside the Castillo de San Jorge, across the Triana Bridge (aka Puente de Isabel II) on the west bank of the river (Mon–Sun 9.30am–3pm; 955 470 255, www.visita sevilla.es). There are information points dotted around the city, many noticeable by their orange glow: the most helpful being at Santa Justa train station and Avenida de la Constitución.

Festivals and events

King's Day

January 6

King's Day or Reyes is the joyous winter holiday celebrating the coming of the wise men in the Catholic calendar (Epiphany). Spaniards exchange their gifts on this day and there is an impressive and very festive parade through the streets of Seville the evening before, with lights, music, dance, food, floats and costumes.

Carnaval

February, week before Lent

While the big Carnaval is most celebrated in Cádiz (worth a trip), you'll likely see groups of costumed performers singing their clever comedic tunes on the streets of Seville throughout the month of February. Just listen for the kazoos.

Semana Santa (Holy Week)

March, week before Easter

You'll find memorable and elaborate Catholic processions of pasos (floats) and penitents throughout the whole city. All culminate with dramatic candlelight processions at dawn on Good Friday, with Easter Day itself more of a quiet occasion.

Bullfighting season

Mid-April

The season for bullfighting is mid-April through to the end of September, with the main corridas staged during the April fair.

Feria de Abril

Last week of April, beginning of May

Seville's week-long fair, celebrated with extraordinary folkloric dress and endless hours of music, dancing, drink and food until the sun comes up. The fairgrounds are located south of Triana, across the bridge from Puerta de Jerez.

Interestellar
May
Seville's biggest music festival, focused on the indie rock scene with some appearances from big-named Spanish pop artists.

Romería del Rocío
Pentecost, mid-May
Horsedrawn carriages and processions converge from all over the south on El Rocío (Huelva). As they pass through Seville, you can catch sights of the decorated carriages, massive bulls and festive costume.

Corpus Christi
Beginning of June
Corpus Christi is a Semana Santa-like procession on an infinitely smaller scale, where the presence of the body of Christ is paraded through the streets by float. The main celebration takes place in the Plaza de San Francisco, which is decorated for the event.

Velá de Santa Ana
End of July
Santa Ana, the patron saint of Triana, is celebrated in the neighbourhood with its own special fair. Stand on the riverfront and watch the entertaining game of La Cucaña, where young men attempt to grab a flag at the end of an oil-slicked log before falling into the water below.

La Liga
Beginning of August
La Liga Spanish soccer season begins with Seville's two rival teams: Sevilla FC, who play in the Sánchez Pizjuán stadium (www.sevillafc.com), and Real Betis, in the Benito Villamarín stadium (www.realbetisbalompie.es).

Feria de San Miguel
End of September
A small fair along the banks of the river, on the Centro Histórico side of the Triana Bridge. Tents are filled with food, drinks and music, and usually lots of dancing as the night goes on. It's also an important moment in the bullfighting calendar.

European Film Festival
November
The European Film Festival is held every year in Seville in various theatres around the city. Films are played in their original language with subtitles in Spanish. Tickets can be purchased individually, or as a festival pass. Regardless, it's a good idea to reserve seats in advance; they get booked up quickly.

Chronology

1.5 million years ago Early humans active at Orce in the province of Granada after arriving from Africa.

25,000 BC Cave dwellers occupy caves in Málaga province.

12,000 BC Cave paintings made at Altamira in Cantabria and dolmens constructed in Catalunya and Málaga.

2500 BC Chalcolithic (Copper Age) sites flourish in Almería.

c.1100 BC Phoenicians found Cádiz.

c.1000 BC Semi-mythical kingdom of Tartessus flourishes in the southwest of the peninsula.

c.9th–4th century BC Celts settle in the north and west of the peninsula.

Greeks establish trading posts along east coast.

600–300 BC Greeks establish trading colonies along the Mediterranean coast.

c.5th century BC Carthage colonizes southern Spain. Celtiberian culture develops, with Greek influence.

c.214 BC Second Punic War with Rome.

210 BC Roman colonization begins.

27 BC Octavian-Augustus becomes the first Roman emperor.

c.409–415 Vandals invade Spain.

c.5th–7th century Visigoths arrive and take control of most of Spain.

711 Moors under Tariq invade and defeat Visigothic King Roderic near Jerez. Seville is conquered in 712. Peninsula conquered in seven years.

722 Pelayo defeats Moors at Covadonga in Asturias in northern Spain marking the start of the Reconquest.

756 Abd-al-Rahman I proclaims Emirate of Córdoba. Great mosque of Córdoba (Mezquita) begun.

c.9th century Kingdoms of Catalunya and Navarra founded.

967 Al-Mansur usurps Caliphal powers of Córdoba Caliphate and forces Christians back into Asturias.

1031 Caliphate disintegrates into *taifas* (petty kingdoms).

1037 Fernando I unites kingdoms of Castile and León-Asturias.

1085 Christians capture Toledo.

1086 Almoravids invade Spain from North Africa.

1147 Invasion by Almohads from Morocco; Seville becomes new Moorish capital in Spain.

1162 Alfonso II unites kingdoms of Aragón and Catalunya.

1212 Almohad advance halted at Las Navas de Tolosa in Andalucía.

1213 Jaime I "El Conquistador" becomes king of Aragón and leads Christian Reconquest of Balearics (1229), Valencia (1238) and Alicante (1266).

1217 Fernando III "El Santo" crowned king of Castile, and retakes Córdoba (1236), Murcia (1241) and Seville (1248).

1469 Castile and Aragón united by the marriage of Isabel and Fernando, Los Reyes Católicos (the Catholic Monarchs).

1492 Fall of Granada, the last Moorish kingdom. "Discovery" of America by Cristóbal Colón (Columbus).

1516 Carlos V succeeds to the throne and becomes the Holy Roman Emperor (1520), inaugurating the Golden Age.

1519 Cortés lands in Mexico.

1532 Pizarro "discovers" Peru.

1556 Accession of Felipe II (d.1598).

1588 British forces defeat the Spanish Armada. Marks Spain's demise as a sea power.

1605 Miguel de Cervantes writes *Don Quijote (Quixote)*, considered the first modern novel.

1609 Expulsion of Moriscos, last remaining Spanish Muslims.

1700 War of Spanish Succession brings Felipe V (1683–1746), a Bourbon, to the throne. British seize Gibraltar.

1808 France occupies Spain. Venezuela declares independence, others follow.

1812 Liberal constitution declared in Cádiz.

1833–39 First Carlist War. Dissolution of the monasteries.

1898 Loss of Cuba, Spain's last American colony.

1923 Primo de Rivera dictatorship. Resigns (1930) due to ill health and popular agitation urges a republic.

1929 Seville hosts the Ibero-American Expo.

1931 King Alfonso XIII is forced out and the Second Republic is declared.

1936 Spanish Civil War begins.

1937 Basque town of Gernika is destroyed by German bombers. Over 1500 civilians are killed.

1939 Civil War ends and Franco dictatorship begins.

1953 US makes economic deal with Franco in return for military bases.

1975 Death of Franco. Spain becomes a constitutional monarchy with Juan Carlos I as king.

1981 Attempted military coup fails; members of parliament are held hostage in the Cortes (Spanish Parliament).

1986 Spain joins the European Union.

1992 Seville hosts the World Expo.

2002 Spain swaps peseta for euro.

2004 Madrid train bombings kill 191 and injure more than 1800, influencing the outcome of the general election held three days later.

2009 Spanish economy enters recession.

2010 Spain wins the FIFA World Cup in South Africa for the first time.

2014 Following royal scandals, King Juan Carlos I abdicates; his son is crowned Felipe VI with consort Queen Letizia.

2017 After sixty years, Basque militant group ETA ends its armed campaign and surrenders its arms caches. Terrorist attack on Barcelona's Ramblas kills sixteen people.

2019 Protestors in Cataluña take to the streets against the imprisonment of Catalan leaders, convicted of sedition.

2020 Covid-19 pandemic forces Spain into strict quarantine lockdown for two months.

2022 Tourism picks up to pre-pandemic rates.

2023 Spain wins the FIFA Women's World Cup in Australia for the first time.

Language

Once you give it a try, Spanish (Castellano or Castilian) is among the easier languages to get a grip on. Unfortunately, you may be surprised that you understand very little in Seville. Andalusians are known for eating their consonants and speaking especially fast and a bit mumbled. "Mas o menos" for example, may sound a bit more like "mah o menoh." English is spoken in hotels and in the more centrally located restaurants and monuments, but wherever you are you'll get a far better reception if you at least try communicating with Spaniards in their own tongue. Being understood, of course, is only half the problem –getting the gist of the reply, often rattled out at a furious pace, may prove far more difficult.

Castilian

The rules of pronunciation are straightforward and, once you get to know them, strictly observed. Unless there's an accent, words ending in d, l, r and z are stressed on the last syllable, all others on the second last. All vowels are pure and short; combinations have predictable results.

A somewhere between the A sound of "back" and that of "father".

E as in "get".

I as in "police".

O as in "hot".

U as in "rule".

C is lisped before E and I; otherwise, hard: cerca is pronounced "thairka" (though in Andalucía many natives pronounce the soft "c" as an "s").

G works the same way, a guttural "H" sound (like the ch in "loch") before E or I, a hard G elsewhere – gigante becomes "higante".

H is always silent.

J the same sound as a guttural G: jamón is pronounced "hamon".

LL sounds like an English Y or LY: tortilla is pronounced "torteeya".

N is as in English unless it has a tilde (accent) over it, when it becomes NY: mañana sounds like "man-yana".

QU is pronounced like an English K.

R is subtly rolled, RR doubly so.

V sounds more like B, vino becoming "beano".

X has an S sound before consonants, normal X before vowels.

Z is the same as a soft C, so cerveza becomes "thairvaitha" (but again much of the south prefers the "s" sound).

Castilian words and phrases

Basics

Yes Sí
No No
Please Por favor
Thank you Gracias
Where Dónde
When Cuando
What Qué
How much Cuánto
This Esto
That Eso
Now Ahora
Later Más tarde
Open Abierto/a
Closed Cerrado/a
With Con
Without Sin
Big Gran(de)
Small Pequeño/a
Hot Caliente
Cold Frío
More Más
Less Menos
Today Hoy
Tomorrow Mañana

Greetings and responses

Hello Hola
Goodbye Adiós
Good morning Buenos días
Good afternoon/night Buenas tardes/noches
See you later Hasta luego
Sorry Lo siento/disculpéme
Excuse me Perdón/Con permiso

How are you? ¿Como está (usted)?
I (don't) understand (No) Entiendo
Not at all/You're welcome De nada
Do you speak English? ¿Habla (usted) inglés?
I (don't) speak Spanish (No) Hablo español

Hotels and transport

I want Quiero
I'd like Quisiera
Could I have...? ¿Me puedes poner...?
Do you have ...? ¿Tiene ...?
the time la hora
a room una habitación
It's for one person (two people) Es para una persona (dos personas)
for one night (one week) para una noche (una semana)
It's fine, how much is it? ¿Está bien, cuánto es?
It's too expensive Es demasiado caro
Don't you have anything cheaper? No tiene algo más barato?
Is there a hostel nearby?   ¿Hay un hostal aquí cerca?
How do I get to ...? ¿Por donde se va a ...?
Left Lzquierda
Right Derecha,
Straight on Todo recto
Where is ...? ¿Dónde está ...?
the bus station la estación de autobuses
the train station la estación de station ferro-carril
the nearest bank el banco mas cercano
the post office el correos/la oficina de correos
the toilet el baño/aseo/servicio
Where does the bus to ... leave from? ¿De dónde sale el autobús para ...?
Is this the train for Mérida? ¿Es este el tren para Mérida?
I'd like a (return) ticket to ... Quisiera un billete (de ida y vuelta) para ...
What time does it leave (arrive in ...)? ¿A qué hora sale (llega a...)?

Numbers and days

one un/uno/una
two dos
three tres
four cuatro
five cinco
six seis
seven siete
eight ocho
nine nueve
ten diez
eleven once
twelve doce
thirteen trece
fourteen catorce
fifteen quince
sixteen diez y seis
twenty veinte
twenty-one veintiuno
thirty treinta
forty cuarenta
fifty cincuenta
sixty sesenta
seventy setenta
eighty ochenta
ninety noventa
one hundred cien(to)
one hundred and one ciento uno
two hundred doscientos
five hundred quinientos
one thousand mil
Monday Lunes
Tuesday Martes
Wednesday Miércoles
Thursday Jueves
Friday Viernes
Saturday Sábado
Sunday Domingo

Menu reader

Basics

Aceite Oil
Ajo Garlic
Arroz Rice
Azúcar Sugar
Huevos Eggs
Mantequilla Butter
Miel Honey
Pan Bread
Picos Small breadsticks
Pimienta Pepper
Sal Salt
Vinagre Vinegar

Meals

Almuerzo/Comida Lunch
Botella Bottle
Carta Menu
Cena Dinner
Comedor/Salón Dining room
Cuchara Spoon
Cuchillo Knife
La cuenta The bill
Desayuno Breakfast
Menú del día Fixed-price set meal
Mesa Table
Platos combinados Mixed plate
Tenedor Fork
Vaso Glass

Fish (pescados)

Anchoas Anchovies (canned)
Anguila/Angulas Eel/Elvers
Atún Tuna
Bacalao Cod (often salt)
Bonito Tuna
Caballa Mackerel
Chanquetes Whitebait
Dorada Bream
Lenguado Sole
Lubina Sea bass
Melva Tuna (usually canned)
Merluza Hake
Mero Grouper
Pez espada Swordfish
Rape Monkfish
Raya Ray skate
Rodaballo Turbot
Rosada Rockfish
Salmonete Mullet
Sardinas Sardines
Trucha Trout

Seafood (mariscos)

Almejas Clams
Arroz con mariscos Rice with seafood
Centollo Spider crab
Chipirones Small squid
Chocos Cuttlefish
Cigalas King prawns
Conchas finas Large scallops
Coquinas Coquina clams
Gambas Prawns/shrimps
Langosta Lobster

Navajas Razor clams
Nécora Sea crab
Ostras Oysters
Paella Classic Valencian dish with saffron
rice, chicken, seafood, etc
Percebes Goose barnacles
Pulpo Octopus
Vieiras/Zamburiñas Scallops

Meat (carne) and poultry (aves)

Abanico, Secreto, Pluma, Presa Cuts of
Ibérico pork
Carillada Pork cheek
Carne de buey Beef
Cerdo Pork
Cerdo ibérico High-quality, black-hoofed
pork
Choto Baby kid
Chuletas Chops
Cochinillo Suckling pig
Codorniz Quail
Cordero Lamb
Escalopa Escalope
Hígado Liver
Jabalí Wild boar
Pato Duck
Pavo Turkey
Pollo Chicken
Riñones Kidneys
Solomillo Sirloin steak
Solomillo de cerdo (ibérico) Pork
tenderloin
Ternera Beef/Veal
Venado Venison

Vegetables (legumbres)

Acelga Chard
Alcachofas Artichokes
Batatas/boniato Sweet potato
Berenjenas Aubergine
Calabacín Summer squash, zucchini
Cebollas Onions
Champiñones/Setas Mushrooms
Coliflor Cauliflower
Espárragos Asparagus
Espinacas Spinach
Lechuga Lettuce
Lentejas Lentils
Nabos Turnips
Patatas/Papas Potatoes

Pepino Cucumber
Pisto manchego Spanish ratatouille
Puerros Leeks
Puré Mashed potato
Remolacha Beet
Repollo/Co Cabbage
Zanahoria Carrot

Fruits (frutas)

Albaricoques Apricots
Cerezas Cherries
Chirimoyas Custard apples
Ciruelas Plums, prunes
Dátiles Dates
Fresas Strawberries
Granada Pomegranate
Higos Figs
Manzanas Apples
Melocotones Peaches
Naranjas Oranges
Peras Pears
Piña Pineapple
Plátanos Bananas
Sandía Watermelon
Toronja/Pomelo Grapefruit
Uvas Grapes

Common terms

al ajillo in garlic
a la brasa grilled over embers
a la parrilla/plancha grilled
al horno baked
al vapor steamed
aliñá (aliñada) marinated or dressed
alioli with garlic mayonnaise
asado roasted
en escabeche in spiced vinegar sauce
en salsa in (usually tomato) sauce
frito fried
guisado casserole, stew
salteado sautéed
rehogado sautéed

Soups (sopas) and starters

Ajo blanco Chilled almond and garlic soup
Caldo Broth
Gazpacho Chilled tomato, peppers and garlic soup
Pimientos rellenos Stuffed peppers
Salmorejo Thick, chilled tomato soup

Cheese

Cheeses (quesos) are on the whole local, though you'll get the hard, salty queso manchego everywhere. Mild to heavily cured sheep's or goat's cheese (queso de oveja/cabra) are even more widely available in the Seville, many of which are made just outside the city or in surrounding towns in Andalucía.

Standard tapas and raciones

Aceitunas Olives
Adobo Marinated fried fish
Albóndigas Meatballs
Aliños Marinated chilled vegetables, sometimes with seafood
Berberechos Cockles
Berenjenas fritas Fried aubergine (usually with cane syrup or honey)
Boquerones Anchovies
Cabrillas Large snails with tomato
Calamares Squid
Caracolas Whelks
Caracoles Snails
Chicharrones Fried pork belly bits
Chicharrones de Cádiz Roasted pork belly, sliced thin
Chocos Deep-fried cuttlefish
Chorizo Spiced sausage, either cooked or dry-cured
Cocido Stew
Costillas Pork ribs
Empanada Savory pastry
Espinacas con garbanzos Spinach with chickpeas
Flamenquín Breaded and fried pork and cheese roll
Gambas (al ajillo) Prawns (cooked in garlic)
Habas con jamón Broad beans with ham
Hígado (de pollo) Liver (chicken liver), usually cooked with onions or garlic
Jamón serrano Cured ham (like Parma ham)
Jamón ibérico Longer cured black-hoofed ham
Jamón ibérico bellota Longer cured ham from black-hoofed acorn-eating pigs (the best)
Langostinos Big, deep-water prawns
Mejillones Mussels, often canned vinegary escabeche
Montadito Hand-held sandwich

Morcilla Blood sausage (black pudding), often with rice or dry-cured
Pavia Fried cod fritter
Patatas alioli Potatoes in garlic mayonnaise
Patatas bravas Fried potatoes with spicy sauce and mayo
Pimientos Bell peppers, usually roasted
Pincho moruno Marinated grilled chicken kabob
Pringá Slow-cooked pork meat mixture
Puchero Pork and garbanzo stew
Pulpo a la Gallega Boiled octopus with paprika
Puntillitas Deep-fried baby squid
Riñones al Jerez Kidneys in sherry
Salchicha Sausage
Salchichón Cured, peppery salami
Salomillo al Whisky Pork loin in garlic whisky sauce
Sepia Cuttlefish, usually fried
Serranito Pork, jamón, fried pepper sandwich
Tabla Charcuterie or cheese board, sometimes cured seafood
Tortilla de camarones Shrimp fritters
Tortilla española Potato omelette

Desserts (postres)

Arroz con leche Rice pudding
Helado Ice cream
Pestiños Crispy fried dough soaked in honey and anise
Pionono Soaked cake topped with brûléed custard
Polvorónes Crumbly cookie made with lard
Rosco Sugar-encrusted cake donut
Roscón de Reyes King's Cake
Tarta de Almendras Almond tart
Tarta de manzana Apple tart
Tocino del Cielo Syrup and egg flan
Torrija French toast soaked in honey, wine, or sprinkled with sugar
Turrón Almond nougat

Drinks

Cafe con leche Espresso with steamed milk
Cortado Espresso with a splash of steamed milk
Cafe solo Espresso shot
Manchado Steamed milk with a stain of espresso

Vino tinto Red wine
Vino blanco White wine
Vinos generosos Sherry wines
Caña Small glass of beer
De barril from the tap (beer)
Botellín Small bottle of beer
Tercio Large bottle of beer
Agua del grifo tap water

Glossary of Spanish and architectural terms

Alameda Park or grassy promenade
Alcazaba Moorish castle
Alcázar Moorish fortified palace
Ayuntamiento Town hall
Azulejo ceramic tilework
Barrio Suburb, quarter, neighbourhood
Bodega Cellar, wine bar or warehouse
Calle Street
Capilla mayor Chapel containing the high altar
Cartuja Carthusian monastery
Castillo Castle
Chiringuito Beach restaurant serving fish, seafood and paella
Convento Monastery or convent
Correos Post office
Corrida de toros Bullfight
Ermita Hermitage
Fortaleza Fortress
Iglesia Church
Mercado Market
Mercadillo Flea market
Mirador Viewpoint
Monasterio Monastery or convent
Muralla City walls
Palacio Aristocratic mansion
Paso Float processed during Catholic festivals like Semana Santa
Paseo Promenade; also the evening stroll thereon
Plaza Square
Plaza de toros Bullring
Puerto Port
Raciones Large plate of tapas, often shared
Sevillana Style of folkloric flamenco partner dance
Sierra Mountain range
Solar Aristocratic town mansion
Turismo Tourist office or tourism

SMALL PRINT

Publishing information
First edition 2024

Distribution
UK, Ireland and Europe
Apa Publications (UK) Ltd; sales@roughguides.com
United States and Canada
Ingram Publisher Services; ips@ingramcontent.com
Australia and New Zealand
Booktopia; retailer@booktopia.com.au
Worldwide
Apa Publications (UK) Ltd; sales@roughguides.com

Special Sales, Content Licensing and CoPublishing
Rough Guides can be purchased in bulk quantities at discounted prices. We can create special editions, personalised jackets and corporate imprints tailored to your needs. sales@roughguides.com.
roughguides.com

Printed in Czech Republic

This book was produced using **Typefi** automated publishing software.

A catalogue record for this book is available from the British Library

The publishers and authors have done their best to ensure the accuracy and currency of all the information in **Pocket Rough Guide Seville**, however, they can accept no responsibility for any loss, injury, or inconvenience sustained by any traveller as a result of information or advice contained in the guide.

Rough Guide credits
Editor: Joanna Reeves
Cartography: Katie Bennett
Picture Editor: Tom Smyth
Layout: Grzegorz Madejak
Original design: Richard Czapnik
Head of DTP and Pre-Press: Rebeka Davies
Head of Publishing: Sarah Clark

Acknowledgements
Megan would like to thank first and foremost the people of Seville: to all of the servers, bartenders, cooks, managers, housekeeping attendants, hotel concierges, artists, street cleaners, gardeners, guides, monument workers and everyone else who works tirelessly to make this city a welcoming place for folks around

the world. Thank you also to the lovely team at Rough Guides, especially editor Jo Reeves. Most importantly, thank you to all my friends and family here in this adopted city of mine, who not only welcomed me with copious hospitality, but plunged me into the intricacies of their beautiful culture. Last but not least, thank you to my husband Carlos, whose profound knowledge, love and support made this guide possible.

SMALL PRINT

Authors

Megan Lloyd is a Texas-born, Seville-based travel, food and drink writer. She has lived full-time in Spain since 2018 and has since become an expert in Spanish culture, travel and gastronomy, with a particular focus on the south. Her work has appeared in publications like Condé Nast Traveler, Bon Appétit, United Airline's Hemispheres, and many more. Follow Megan on Instagram at @meganfranceslloyd.

Joanna Reeves is a Sussex-based travel writer and editor who has updated several European Rough Guides, including the *Rough Guide to England*, *Pocket Rough Guide Porto* and *Rough Guide Mini Bologna*. She is also the editor of the brand-new *Rough Guide to Slow Travel in Europe*.

Help us update

We've gone to a lot of effort to ensure that this edition of the **Pocket Rough Guide Seville** is accurate and up-to-date. However, things change – places get "discovered", opening hours are notoriously fickle, restaurants and rooms raise prices or lower standards. If you feel we've got it wrong or left something out, we'd like to know, and if you can remember the address, the price, the hours, the phone number, so much the better.

Please send your comments with the subject line "**Pocket Rough Guide Seville Update**" to mail@uk.roughguides.com. We'll credit all contributions and send a copy of the next edition (or any other Rough Guide if you prefer) for the very best emails.

Photo credits

(Key: T-top; C-centre; B-bottom; L-left; R-right)

Antonio Arévalo/www.fotowork.es 110/111
Javier Peñas/Noor 97
La Casa del Tigre 22B
Lolo Vasco/ Tramagestión/Turismo Andaluz 41, 49, 101, 102
Pura Vida Terraza 40
Shutterstock 1, 2TL, 2BL, 2C, 2BR, 4, 5, 6, 7, 8, 12, 13T, 13B, 14/15T, 14BL, 14/15B, 15C, 16B, 16T, 17B, 17T, 18B, 18T, 19B, 19T, 20T, 20C, 21T, 21C, 21B,

22T, 22C, 23T, 23C, 23B, 24/25, 26, 27, 31, 32, 33, 34, 35, 36, 37, 38, 39, 42, 43, 45, 46, 47, 48, 50, 51, 53, 54, 55, 56, 57, 59, 60, 61, 62, 63, 64, 65, 67, 68, 69, 71, 72, 73, 74, 75, 77, 78, 79, 80, 82, 83, 84, 85, 86, 88, 89, 91, 92, 93, 94, 95, 96, 98, 99, 100, 104, 105, 107, 108, 109, 120/121
Sobretablas 20B
Turismo Andaluz 81

Cover: Plaza Espana **May Lana/Shutterstock**

Index

A

accessible travel 124
accommodation 112
  Casa Romana Hotel Boutique 115
  Cavalta Boutique Hotel 114
  El Cicerone de Sevilla 114
  El Naranjito de Triana 115
  Eurostars Guadalquivir 114
  Exe Sevilla Macarena 115
  H10 Casa de la Plata 112
  H10 Corregidor Boutique Hotel 115
  Halo Boutique Hotel Sevilla 113
  Hostal Puerta Carmona 113
  Hotel Alcázar 114
  Hotel Alfonso XIII 113
  Hotel Amadeus 113
  Hotel Boutique Casa de Colón 112
  Hotel Murillo 113
  Hotel Pasarela 114
  Hotel Ribera de Triana 114
  Hotel Sacristía de Santa Ana 115
  Hotel Simón 113
  Hotel Zaida 113
  Jardin de la Alameda Boutique 115
  La Banda Rooftop Hostel 112
  La Casa del Maestro 113
  Las Casas de la Judería 114
  Las Casas del Rey de Baeza 112
  Meliá Sevilla 114
  Noches en Triana 115
  Oasis Backpackers Hostel 113
  Pájaro Rebelde 115
  Patio de Alameda 116
  Pensión Pérez Montilla 114
  Santacruz Hostal Plaza 114
  Santiago 15 Casa Palacio 113
  The Corner House 115
  TOC Hostel 113
  Triana Backpackers Hostel 115
  Triana Boutique Apartments 115
  Zenit Sevilla 115
accommodation (by area)
  Alameda 115
  Aracena 116
  Cádiz 119
  Carmona 117
  Centro Histórico 112
  Córdoba 117
  Grazalema 116
  Jerez de la Frontera 118
  Ronda 116
  Santa Cruz 113
  Sur 114
  Triana and the Guadalquivir 114

Ubrique 116
accommodation price codes 112
Acinipo 77
Acuario de Sevilla (Aquarium of Seville) 54
addresses 124
Alameda de Hércules 65
Alameda, San Lorenzo and Macarena 64
Alcázar 32
Antigua Fábrica de Tabacos (Royal Tobacco Factory) 50
Aracena 81
Archivo de Indias 30
Arcos de la Frontera 80
arrival 122
Ayuntamiento 32

B

bars and clubs
  1987 Bar 71
  Bestiario 40
  Carambolo 71
  Casa Vizcaíno 71
  Fun Club 71
  Kiosko Líbano 55
  KOKO 40
  Lama La Uva 40
  Maruja Melón 62
  Muelle New York 55
  O'Clock Club & Bar 40
  Pura Vida Terraza 40
  The Holiday 71
bars and clubs (by area)
  Alameda, San Lorenzo and Macarena 71
  Jerez de la Frontera 103
bars and clubs(by area)
  Centro Histórico 40
  Río Guadalquivir and Triana 62
  Sur 55
Basílica de Jesus del Gran Poder 67
bike 123
bus 123
by bus 122
by car 122
by plane 122
by train 122

C

CAAC 61
Cádiz 104
  Catedral Nueva 107
  getting to 107
  Hospital de Mujeres 108

  Iglesia Santa Cruz 107
  La Viña 104
  Mercado Central 108
  Museo de Cádiz 105
  Plaza de las Flores 108
  Santa Cueva 108
cafés
  Confitería La Campana 38
  El Comercio 38
  El Viajero Sedentario 70
cafés (by area)
  Alameda, San Lorenzo and Macarena 70
  Centro Histórico 38
Capilla de los Marineros 60
Carmona 82
Casa de Pilatos 43
Castilian 130
  menu reader 131
  words and phrases 130
Castillo de San Jorge 60
Catedral 26
Centro Histórico 26
children 124
chronology 127
cinema 124
Convent cookies 5
Córdoba 86
  Alcázar de los Reyes Cristianos 91
  Casa Andalusí 92
  Casa de Sefarad 92
  getting to 87
  La Judería 92
  Medina Azahara 94
  Mezquita 87
  Museo Arqueológico 92
  Museo Taurino 92
  Palacio del Marqués de Viana 94
  Plaza de la Corredera 91
  Plaza del Potro 93
  pretty patios 90
  Sinagoga 92
  Torre de la Calahorra 90
crime and emergencies 124
Cueva de la Pileta 78

D

day-trips 72
Directory A–Z 124
drinking 9

E

eating 9
eating out price codes 125

NOTES

NOTES